BARRON'S BOOK NOTES

JAMES JOYCE'S

A Portrait of the Artist as a Young Man

BY

Arlette Brauer

SERIES COORDINATOR

Murray Bromberg
Principal, Wang High School of Queens
Holliswood, New York

Past President
High School Principals Association of New York City

GW00545328

BARRON'S EDUCATIONAL SERIES, INC.

ACKNOWLEDGMENTS

Our thanks to Milton Katz and Julius Liebb for their contribution to the *Book Notes* series.

© Copyright 1985 by Barron's Educational Series, Inc.

All inquiries should be addressed to:
Barron's Educational Series, Inc.
250 Wireless Boulevard
Hauppauge, New York 11788

Library of Congress Catalog Card No. 85-4079

International Standard Book No. 0-8120-3535-6

Library of Congress Cataloging in Publication Data
Brauer, Arlette.
   James Joyce's Portrait of the artist as a young man.

   (Barron's book notes)
   Bibliography: p. 111
Summary: A guide to reading "A Portrait of the Artist
as a Young Man" with a critical and appreciative mind
encouraging analysis of plot, style, form, and structure.
Also includes background on the author's life and times,
sample tests, term paper suggestions, and a reading list.
   1. Joyce, James, 1882–1941. Portrait of the artist
as a young man. [1. Joyce, James, 1882–1941. Portrait
of the artist as a young man. 2. English literature—
History and criticism] I. Title. II. Series.
PR6019.09P64335 1985   823'.912   85-4079
ISBN 0-8120-3535-6

PRINTED IN THE UNITED STATES OF AMERICA

3456   550   98765432

CONTENTS

Advisory Board   iv

How to Use This Book   v

THE AUTHOR AND HIS TIMES   1

THE NOVEL   10

The Plot   10

The Characters   13

Other Elements   24

    Setting   24

    Catholic Ireland   25

    Irish Nationalism   28

    The Daedalus Myth   30

    Themes   32

    Style   36

    Point of View   39

    Form and Structure   41

The Story   43

A STEP BEYOND   100

Tests and Answers   100

Term Paper Ideas and other Topics
  for Writing   110

Further Reading   111

    Critical Works   111

    Author's Other Works   113

Glossary   113

The Critics   117

ADVISORY BOARD

HOW TO USE THIS BOOK

You have to know how to approach literature in order to get the most out of it. This *Barron's Book Notes* volume follows a plan based on methods used by some of the best students to read a work of literature.

Begin with the guide's section on the author's life and times. As you read, try to form a clear picture of the author's personality, circumstances, and motives for writing the work. This background usually will make it easier for you to hear the author's tone of voice, and follow where the author is heading.

Then go over the rest of the introductory material—such sections as those on the plot, characters, setting, themes, and style of the work. Underline, or write down in your notebook, particular things to watch for, such as contrasts between characters and repeated literary devices. At this point, you may want to develop a system of symbols to use in marking your text as you read. (Of course, you should only mark up a book you own, not one that belongs to another person or a school.) Perhaps you will want to use a different letter for each character's name, a different number for each major theme of the book, a different color for each important symbol or literary device. Be prepared to mark up the pages of your book as you read. Put your marks in the margins so you can find them again easily.

Now comes the moment you've been waiting for— the time to start reading the work of literature. You may want to put aside your *Barron's Book Notes* volume until you've read the work all the way through. Or you may want to alternate, reading the *Book Notes* analysis of each section as soon as you have finished reading the corresponding part of the original. Before you move on, reread crucial passages you don't fully understand. (Don't take this guide's analysis for granted—make up your own mind as to what the work means.)

Once you've finished the whole work of literature, you may want to review it right away, so you can firm up your ideas about what it means. You may want to leaf through the book concentrating on passages you marked in reference to one character or one theme. This is also a good time to reread the *Book Notes* introductory material, which pulls together insights on specific topics.

When it comes time to prepare for a test or to write a paper, you'll already have formed ideas about the work. You'll be able to go back through it, refreshing your memory as to the author's exact words and perspective, so that you can support your opinions with evidence drawn straight from the work. Patterns will emerge, and ideas will fall into place; your essay question or term paper will almost write itself. Give yourself a dry run with one of the sample tests in the guide. These tests present both multiple-choice and essay questions. An accompanying section gives answers to the multiple-choice questions as well as suggestions for writing the essays. If you have to select a term paper topic, you may choose one from the list of suggestions in this book. This guide also provides you with a reading list, to help you when you start research for a term paper, and a selection of provocative comments by critics, to spark your thinking before you write.

THE AUTHOR
AND HIS TIMES

"Silence, exile, and cunning."—these are weapons Stephen Dedalus chooses in *A Portrait of the Artist as a Young Man*. And these, too, were weapons that its author, James Joyce, used against a hostile world.

Like his fictional hero, Stephen, the young Joyce felt stifled by the narrow interests, religious pressures, and political squabbles of turn-of-the-century Ireland. In 1904, when he was twenty-two, he left his family, the Roman Catholic Church, and the "dull torpor" of Dublin for the European continent to become a writer. With brief exceptions, he was to remain away from Ireland for the rest of his life.

It was a bold move for several reasons. In spite of his need to break away from constrictions on his development as a writer, Joyce had always been close to his family. He still admired the intellectual and artistic aspects of the Roman Catholic tradition that had nurtured him. And the city of Dublin was in his soul. (Asked later how long he had been away from Dublin, he answered: "Have I ever left it?")

But Joyce did achieve his literary goal in exile. The artistic climate of continental Europe encouraged experiment. With cunning (skillfulness) and hard work, Joyce developed his own literary voice. He labored for ten years on *Portrait of the Artist*, the fictionalized account of his youth. When it appeared in book form in 1916, twelve years after

Joyce's flight from Ireland, it created a sensation. Joyce was hailed as an important new force in literature.

Portrait of the Artist is usually read as an autobiography, and many of the incidents in it come from Joyce's youth. But don't assume that he was exactly like his sober hero, Stephen Dedalus. Joyce's younger brother Stanislaus, with whom he was very close, called *Portrait of the Artist* "a lying autobiography and a raking satire." The book should be read as a work of art, not a documentary record. Joyce transformed autobiography into fiction by selecting, sifting, and reconstructing scenes from his own life to create a portrait of Stephen Dedalus, a sensitive and serious young boy who gradually defines himself as an artist.

Still, Joyce and Stephen have much in common. Both were indelibly marked by their upbringing in drab, proud, Catholic Dublin, a city that harbored dreams of being the capital of an independent nation but which in reality was a backwater ruled by England. Like Stephen, Joyce was the eldest son of a family that slid rapidly down the social and economic ladder. When Joyce was born in 1882, the family was still comfortably off. But its income dwindled fast after Joyce's sociable, witty, hard-drinking father, John Stanislaus, lost his political job—as Stephen's father Simon loses his—after the fall of the Irish leader and promoter of independence Charles Stewart Parnell. Although the loss of the post was not directly related to Parnell's fall, Joyce's father worshiped "the uncrowned king of Ireland" and blamed his loss on anti-Parnell forces like the Roman Catholic Church. (Joyce portrays the kind of strong emotions Parnell stirred up in the Christmas dinner scene in Chapter One of *Portrait of the Artist*.) Like Simon Dedalus, the jobless John Stanislaus Joyce was forced to move his family frequently, often leaving rent bills unpaid.

Joyce, though, seems to have taken a more cheerful view of his family problems, and to have shown more patience with his irresponsible father, than did his fictional hero. He seems to have inherited some of his father's temperament; he could clown at times, and he laughed so readily he was called "Sunny Jim." He also inherited a tenor voice good enough to make him consider a concert career. Many believe that musical talent is responsible for Joyce's gift for language.

Joyce's father was determined that his son have the finest possible education, and though precarious family finances forced the boy to move from school to school, he received a rigorous Jesuit education. In *Portrait of the Artist* Joyce relives through Stephen the intellectual and emotional struggles that came with his schooling. Joyce's classmates admired the rebellious brilliance that questioned authority, but—like some bright students whom you may know—he remained an outsider, socially and intellectually.

The religious training he received in the Jesuit schools also shaped Joyce, giving him first a faith to believe in and then a weight to rebel against. Like Stephen, he was for a time devoutly religious—then found that other attractions prevailed. By age fourteen he had begun his sexual life furtively in Dublin brothels, and though he was temporarily overwhelmed with remorse after a religious retreat held at his Catholic school, he soon saw that he could not lead the life of virtuous obedience demanded of a priest. Instead, he exchanged religious devotion for devotion to writing.

As a student at University College in Dublin, Joyce studied Latin and modern languages. Although the Gaelic League and other groups were hoping to achieve Irish cultural independence from Great Britain by promoting Irish literature and language, the nonconformist Joyce spurned them. He felt closer to the less provincial trends developing in continental Europe. He memorized whole pages of Gustave Flaubert, the French pioneer of psychological realism and author of *Madame Bovary*, whose precision of style and observation he envied. He also admired the Norwegian playwright Henrik Ibsen, who shocked the world by introducing previously forbidden subjects like venereal disease and immorality among "respectable" citizens in his works. Both these writers drew, as Joyce would, on *all* parts of life—the beautiful, the sordid, and the commonplace.

But realism wasn't the only influence on the young Joyce. The subtle and suggestive poetic imagery of French poets like Stéphane Mallarmé and Arthur Rimbaud, who used symbols to convey shades of meaning, appealed to his love for the musicality of words and for the power of words to evoke unexpected psychological associations. Their example, too, is followed in *Portrait of the Artist*.

Before Joyce had left the university he had already written several essays—one of them on Ibsen—and he had formulated the core of his own theory of art, a theory similar to Stephen's in Chapter Five. The renowned Irish poet William Butler Yeats was impressed by the unkempt but precocious youth, and tried to draw Joyce into the ranks of Irish intellectuals. But once again the arrogant newcomer rejected his homeland, choosing to stay aloof because he felt Yeats and his group viewed the Irish past too romantically and viewed its present with too much nationalism.

Instead, at the age of twenty, Joyce did what Stephen Dedalus is about to do at the novel's end, and turned away from his family, his country, and his church. He ran off to the continent. In 1903 he returned to Ireland to visit his dying mother, but soon after her death (1904) he was again bound for Europe, accompanied by the chambermaid with whom he had fallen in love, Nora Barnacle. The uneducated, sensual Nora seemed an unlikely mate for Joyce, but she proved (despite Joyce's cranky suspicions of her) to be a loyal, lifetime companion.

In Trieste (then a cosmopolitan city of Austria-Hungary), Joyce wrote incessantly and eked out a living teaching English. He put together *Dubliners*, a group of stories based on brief experiences he called "epiphanies." For Joyce, who believed in "the significance of trivial things," an epiphany was a moment of spiritual revelation sparked by a seemingly insignificant detail. A chance word, a particular gesture or situation could suddenly reveal a significant truth about an entire life.

He also continued work on a novel he had started in Ireland. The first, brief version of what we know as *A Portrait of the Artist as a Young Man* had been curtly rejected in 1904, before Joyce left Ireland. "I can't print what I can't understand," wrote the British editor who refused it. Undaunted, Joyce expanded the story to nearly one thousand pages. It now bore the title *Stephen Hero*, and was a conventional Bildungsroman—a novel about a young man's moral and psychological development. Other examples of such novels might include D. H. Lawrence's *Sons and Lovers* (1913) or Samuel Butler's *The Way of All Flesh* (1903). (Some critics would be more specific and call *Stephen Hero* and *A Portrait of the Artist* Künstlerromane—novels about the development of young artists.)

Then, dissatisfied, Joyce decided to recast his novel into a shorter, more original form. The final version of *Portrait of the Artist* was stalled by British censorship and it was not until 1914 that Joyce, with the help of Yeats and the American poet Ezra Pound, was able to get it printed in serial form in a "little review," *The Egoist*. *Dubliners*, long delayed by printers' boycotts because of its supposed offensiveness, also appeared the same year. In 1916 *Portrait of the Artist* was published in book form in England and the United States, thanks only to the efforts of Harriet Weaver, editor of *The Egoist*, and Joyce's faithful financial and moral supporter.

When *Portrait of the Artist* did appear, critical reaction was mixed. It was called "garbage" and "brilliant but nasty," among other things. Some readers objected to the graphic physical description, the irreverent treatment of religious matters, the obscurity of its symbolism, and its experimental style. But it was also praised by others as the most exciting English prose of the new century. Joyce, who had fled to neutral Switzerland at the outbreak of World War I, was hailed as "a new writer with a new form" who had broken with the tradition of the English novel.

What sets *Portrait of the Artist* apart from other confessional novels about the development of a creative young man, like D.H. Lawrence's *Sons and Lovers* and Samuel Butler's *The Way of All Flesh* is that the action takes place mainly in the mind of the central character. To portray that mind, Joyce began to develop a technique called the interior monologue, or stream of consciousness, in which he quoted directly the random, unshaped thoughts of his hero. Joyce used this technique sparingly in *Portrait of the Artist*; he exploited it more fully in his later novels.

Portrait of the Artist also differs from more conventional novels because it doesn't show Stephen Dedalus' development in a straightforward chronological progression. Nor do you see it through easily understood flashbacks to the past. Instead Joyce presents a series of episodes that at first may seem unconnected but which in fact are held together by use of language, images, and symbols. Joyce's language changes as Stephen moves from infancy to manhood. The boy who is "nicens little baby tuckoo" becomes the proud young artist who writes in his diary brave promises about forging "the uncreated conscience of my race." Images and symbols are repeated to reveal Stephen's innermost feelings. For example, a rose, or rose color, represents a yearning for romantic love and beauty; the color yellow a revulsion from sordid reality; and birds or flight, an aspiration to creative freedom (and, less often, the threat of punishment and loss of freedom). Such images often relate to larger motifs drawn from religion, philosophy, and myth. Joyce framed his novel in a superstructure of myth (see the section on the Daedalus myth) to relate his hero's personal experience to a universal story of creativity, daring, pride, and self-discovery.

This constellation of words, images, and ideas gives *Portrait of the Artist* a complex texture that offers you far more than a surface telling of Stephen Dedalus' story ever could. It's not easy to explore all the layers of the novel. Joyce removes familiar guideposts. Cause and effect is lost; scenes melt into one another, and the passage of time is not specified. Joyce doesn't explain the many references to places, ideas, and historical events that fill Stephen's mind. It's up to you to make the connections. But if you do, you'll find the effort worthwhile. You'll be participating with Stephen Dedalus in his journey of self-discovery.

After *Portrait of the Artist*, Joyce went even further in transforming the novel in his later works, *Ulysses* and *Finnegans Wake*. Both are virtually plotless and try to reflect the inner workings of the mind in language that demands much from the reader. Stephen Dedalus appears again, though in a secondary role, as a struggling young writer in *Ulysses*. This epic novel connects one day's wanderings of Leopold Bloom, a Jewish Dubliner, with the twenty-year wanderings of the ancient Greek hero Ulysses recounted in Homer's *Odyssey*. *Ulysses* is in some ways a continuation of *Portrait of the Artist*.

Again, no English publisher would print *Ulysses* because of its sexual explicitness and earthy language. It was printed privately in Paris in 1922. Although its early chapters were published serially in the United States, further publication was banned and it was not legally available in the United States again until 1933, when a historic decision written by United States District Judge John Woolsey ruled that it was not obscene.

By then Joyce was living in Paris, an international celebrity and the acknowledged master of the modern literary movement. But even his warmest admirers cooled when *Finnegans Wake* was published in 1939. He was disheartened by the hostile reactions to the extremely obscure language and references in what he felt was his masterwork, the depiction of a cosmic world, built from the dreams of one man in the course of a night's sleep.

Joyce was also increasingly depressed by his failing eyesight, as well as his daughter Lucia's mental illness. His reliance on alcohol increased. Once again a world war sent him into exile in neutral Switzerland. Joyce died in Zurich in 1941.

James Joyce had lived to write. He became a priest of art, as he (Stephen) had promised in *Portrait of the Artist*. Because of his original use of language to tell a story that simultaneously combined mankind's great myths, individual human psychology, and the details of everyday life, Joyce is now held by many to be the most influential prose writer of this century. His influence was felt by many others, including Virginia Woolf, T. S. Eliot, William Faulkner, Thomas Wolfe, and Samuel Beckett. He has left his mark on any writer who uses the stream-of-consciousness technique (see the section on Style), or employs language in a fresh and punning way. And for many writers, like the Anglo-American poet T. S. Eliot, his use of myth to give shape to the chaos of modern life had "the importance of a scientific discovery."

THE NOVEL

The Plot

A Portrait of the Artist as a Young Man opens with the earliest childhood memories of its hero, Stephen Dedalus. Some of these memories are happy and musical. Others hold terror. His governess threatens that if he does not apologize for a mysterious misdeed, eagles will pull out his eyes. This is the first time—but not the last—the sensitive and gifted boy will be pressed to conform to the ways of his world, Roman Catholic Dublin in the late nineteenth century.

Stephen becomes one of the best students at the fashionable boarding school, Clongowes Wood College. Socially, however, he is an outsider, bullied by the other boys. When he returns home to spend Christmas with his family, the holiday proves a disappointment. The festive dinner is disrupted by a bitter argument over Ireland's political idol, Charles Stewart Parnell, whose affair with a married woman has divided both the nation and Stephen's home. His father, Simon; a dinner guest, John Casey; and his governess, Dante Riordan, go at each other's throats. The small boy is dismayed to see his hero, Parnell, attacked, and to see such hate and intolerance among the adults he has been told to respect.

Back at school, Stephen learns that men of God can also behave with cruel injustice when the harsh Father Dolan punishes him unfairly. The outraged Stephen musters enough courage to complain directly to the school's head, Father Conmee, who promises to straighten out the "mistake" with Dolan. The exultant Stephen enjoys a moment of triumph as his schoolmates salute his spunk. But he learns later that Conmee and Dolan merely had a good laugh at his expense.

The Dedalus family suffers the first of many financial reverses and can no longer afford to send Stephen to Clongowes. He goes instead to Belvedere College, a Jesuit school, on scholarship. There he is singled out for his writing skill and discovers the world of books. He is chosen to lead one of the college's two religious brotherhoods. Yet, as before, he feels alienated from the other students. His classmates respect him, but also resent him.

Stephen grows estranged from his family as well. During a trip to Cork, a city on the southern coast of Ireland, his father's drunken bragging embarrasses him, and he is forced to face the fact that Simon Dedalus is a failure who has squandered the family's income. The Dedalus family sinks lower into poverty. The prize money Stephen wins for earning high marks on national exams occasionally helps to brighten a dreary life, but when the money is spent the family's troubles return. He is left isolated from his uncultured parents, feeling not like their true son but like a foster child.

Stephen is also tormented by wild romantic and sexual longings. He focuses these feelings on a young woman, called E. C. or Emma, for whom he has written some verses. But Emma disappoints him when she doesn't wait after he has finished a performance of a school play. The restless, moody lad, now about fourteen, finally satisfies his sexual urges in the arms of a prostitute.

Soon Stephen is regularly visiting Dublin's red-light district and exulting in what he feels is his liberation. He prides himself on not going to confession or to Mass. But guilt lurks under his swagger. The fiery sermons of a Jesuit priest, Father Arnall, evoke the tortures of a Hell to which Stephen fears he may be condemned. In an agony of remorse, he attends confession and returns home, feeling holy and happy.

Stephen's new piety seems so heartfelt that the director of his school gives him the opportunity to join the Jesuits. He finds the vision of priestly knowledge and power briefly tempting, but then rejects it because he prefers "the disorder and misrule" of a nonreligious life to the austere and bloodless order of the priesthood. His true calling, he believes, is to the world of the intellect. As he walks along the shore of Dublin Bay, he spies a girl wading. She seems to him as free and proud as a seabird, and she becomes a symbol of the new creative life he hopes to lead.

Stephen's years at University College reinforce his decision to become a great writer. While his classmates concentrate their energies on Irish politics and culture, Stephen buries himself in his own personal artistic theories and in his poetry. His self-absorbed brilliance causes his friends to consider him an intellectual freak. In turn he feels superior to them.

Romantic and sexual longings still trouble him. When he believes Emma is flirting with a young priest, he grows jealous and convinces himself that she is unworthy. Yet in his fantasies, he continues to transform her into an erotic temptress.

Proudly, regretfully, Stephen sees that he has made himself a stranger to the world that was his at birth—to his family, to Dublin, to Ireland, to Catholicism. He can no longer believe in them, and he proclaims that he can no longer serve what he does not believe in. The artistic and intellectual world beyond Ireland beckons to him. Like the mythic Greek hero, Daedalus, whose name Stephen's recalls, Stephen Dedalus seeks to fly from the forces that have entrapped him. Will he fail or will he succeed? It is not clear. But he is ready to sail to the continent, there to begin a new life as a writer.

The Characters

A Portrait of the Artist as a Young Man contains a large cast of characters. But the central figure, Stephen Dedalus, is by far the most important. Of the others, only two play major roles throughout the novel—Stephen's father, Simon, and his mother, May.

MAJOR CHARACTERS
Stephen Dedalus
A Portrait of the Artist as a Young Man is above all a portrait of Stephen Dedalus. It is through Stephen that you see his world, and it is his development from sensitive child to rebellious young man that forms the plot of the novel.

There are many Stephens, often contradictory. He is fearful yet bold, insecure yet proud, lonely and at the same time afraid of love. One Stephen is a romantic who daydreams of swashbuckling heroes and virginal heroines. The other is a realist at home on Dublin's most sordid streets. One Stephen is too shy to kiss the young lady he yearns for. The other readily turns to prostitutes to satisfy his sexual urges. One is a timid outsider bullied

by his classmates. The other is courageous enough
to confront and question authority. One devoutly
hopes to become a priest. The other cynically rejects religion.

Stephen loves his mother, yet eventually hurts
her by rejecting her Catholic faith. Taught to re-
vere his father, he can't help but see that Simon
Dedalus is a drunken failure. Unhappy as a per-
petual outsider, he lacks the warmth to engage in
true friendship. "Have you never loved anyone?"
his fellow student, Cranly, asks him. "I tried to
love God," Stephen replies. "It seems now I failed."

The force that eventually unites these contradictory Stephens is his overwhelming desire to become an artist, to create. At the novel's opening
you see him as an infant artist who sings "his song."
Eventually you'll see him expand that song into
poetry and theories of art. At the book's end he
has made art his religion, and he abandons family,
Catholicism, and country to worship it.

The name Joyce gave his hero underscores this
aspect of his character. His first name comes from
St. Stephen, the first Christian martyr; many readers have seen Stephen as a martyr to his art. His
last name comes from the great inventor of Greek
myth, Daedalus, whose mazes and waxen wings
are the kind of splendid artistic creations Stephen
hopes to equal in his writing.

Just as Stephen is a contradictory figure, you
may have contradictory feelings about him. You
can believe that he is a brilliant artist who must
flee dull, uncultured Dublin at any cost. You can
admire his intelligence and courage. You can consider his art well worthy of martyrdom, and consider that it merits comparison with Daedalus'
achievements. His theories and poems are, if not

masterpieces, at least the works of a man who may someday create a masterpiece. Indeed, you can believe that Stephen may grow up to be very much like the James Joyce who wrote *Portrait of the Artist.*

On the other hand, you can agree with the readers who call Stephen a supreme egotist, "a posturing, unproven esthete [lover of beauty]," a self-centered snob who has succumbed to the sin of pride. "You are wrapped up in yourself," says his friend MacCann. You can believe, as some readers do, that Stephen's artistic theories and his works of poetry are at most the products of a clever but shallow mind. Stephen may martyr himself for art, but his martyrdom will be worth nothing because he is too self-absorbed to be a great artist. He is not Daedalus; instead he resembles Daedalus' son, Icarus, who, wearing his father's wings, soared too near the sun and died as a result of foolishness and pride.

Or you can take other views. Perhaps Joyce makes fun of Stephen's pretensions while still admiring the bravery that accompanies them. Perhaps Joyce feels sympathy for Stephen's struggles but also feels obliged to mock the less admirable aspects of his hero's character—because he shared those character traits himself.

The title of the novel contains two hints you may want to keep in mind as you make your judgment of Stephen.

1. The novel is a portrait of the artist *as a young man.* Joyce himself said to a friend that his artist was not fully formed yet. Young men often take themselves, and their rebellions, too seriously. Yet they may gain wisdom as they grow older.

2. The novel is *a* portrait, not *the* portrait, of

the artist. Perhaps this is an admission that the book gives only one version of Stephen. Other portraits might add other information and focus on different aspects of his personality.

At the end of *Portrait of the Artist*, will Stephen fly or fall? Joyce does not say. A later work, *Ulysses*, is in part a continuation of Stephen's story, but even in this work Stephen's final fate is not certain. With his complexities and contradictions, Stephen seems more like a living human being than a figure from a book. And who can know everything about another human being? Who can predict with complete certainty what that human being's fate will be?

Simon Dedalus

"A medical student, an oarsman, a tenor, an amateur actor, a shouting politician . . . a drinker, a good fellow, a story teller, somebody's secretary, something in a distillery, a taxgatherer, a bankrupt and at present a praiser of his own past."

That's how Stephen describes his father, Simon Dedalus, toward the end of the novel. *Portrait of the Artist* is a book of discoveries, and one of the most important discoveries Stephen must make is this: what kind of man is his father? Like most sons, he must measure his father in order to measure himself.

Simon Dedalus' character is revealed gradually from the first chapter of the novel to the last. To the infant Stephen he is just a hairy face. A slightly older Stephen knows he is a "gentleman." During the Christmas dinner in Chapter One, you see that Simon can be a genial but argumentative host. In Chapter Two you see that while he may fall from respectability himself, he still believes in it for others.

Stephen must attend an upper-class school run by
the Jesuits, not the Christian Brothers' school that
caters to the lower-class Irish—though Simon is
rapidly becoming part of that class.

As the novel progresses, Simon seems to represent both what is admirable about Ireland and
what is destructive. Simon is a good fellow, a fine
talker, a lover of politics and witty argument. But
he is an irresponsible head of a family, incapable
of keeping a job, saving money, or refusing a drink.

Stephen feels alienated both from his father's
strengths and from his weaknesses. He feels superior to Simon's irresponsibility. But he envies his
father's robustness, gregariousness, and warmth.
When in a bar Simon declares that in his youth he
was a better man than Stephen is now, part of
Stephen fears his father's judgment is correct.

As time goes on, Simon drinks more heavily and
leads his family deeper into poverty. A failure in
the present, he lives in the past. Stephen realizes
that to grow he must reject his biological father and
adopt a spiritual father who will guide him in
his art. He chooses Daedalus, the father and creator of Greek myth. And it's Daedalus, not Simon,
whom Stephen calls "old father," in the final lines
of the book.

May Dedalus

Important as she is in Stephen's thoughts, Stephen's mother, May, is a shadowy figure. She's a
dutiful wife who endures the hardship brought on
by her husband's folly, and who tries to keep peace
within her divided, declining family.

A devout Catholic, Mrs. Dedalus represents to
Stephen the warmth and security a mother can
offer and also the security offered by the Church.

In his mind she is often merged with the Virgin Mary. But he also links her to what he sees as the rigidity and narrow-mindedness of the Catholic Church in Ireland.

Inevitably, as Stephen moves away from the Church he moves away from his mother. The first wedge is driven when he refuses to become a priest, embarking instead on an educational course she considers dangerous.

Yet in the end she is forgiving. Nor is Stephen able to reject her as completely as he does so much else in his life. He notes in his journal that she is putting his "new second-hand clothes" in order for his departure. And she prays he will learn "away from home and friends what the heart is."

OTHER MEMBERS OF THE DEDALUS FAMILY CIRCLE

The Dedalus Children

Stephen's brothers and sisters—there were ten— appear only briefly. He is not close to them and is not even sure how many his mother has had altogether.

Uncle Charles

Stephen's great uncle is one of the few adults drawn with humor and real affection. The genial old codger may have wasted a fortune, but he keeps his dignity—even when exiled to the outhouse where, sporting a tall black hat and singing Irish ballads, he smokes his foul black tobacco. With his carefree talkativeness, Uncle Charles may remind you of Simon Dedalus. Yet Stephen accepts him as he doesn't accept his father. Perhaps it's because, like children, elderly great uncles are permitted to be a little irresponsible while breadwinners of large families are not.

Uncle Charles and his friends are part of Stephen's happy Blackrock summer. Stephen enjoys hearing the old man talk about Irish politics, athletics, and family lore. He seems to represent a happy side of Ireland and of the Dedalus clan you don't see elsewhere. Yet the glories he speaks of are all in the past. And soon he himself is sliding into senility. If you view Uncle Charles both as a colorful character in his own right and as a symbol of a family and a nation, you may suspect that Joyce wants you to see that Ireland, and the Dedalus family, are enduring a decline similar to Uncle Charles'.

Dante Riordan

Stephen's governess, Dante, is an intelligent, well-informed woman of strong convictions and an ardent Irish nationalist. Her hair brushes sport the colors of her political heroes but she strips the colors off when the politicians lose her favor.

Most of all, Dante is a fervent Catholic, a devout believer who almost became a nun. You can see her either as a good Church member or as a religious bigot. When her hero, the nationalist Parnell, is condemned by the Church, she rejects him. The Christmas dinner scene is proof of her strong feelings. Her rigidity is a symbol of the kind of Catholic thinking against which Stephen rebels.

John Casey

Casey, a close friend of the family, is a loyal follower of Parnell. John has even gone to jail because of involvement in pro-Parnell demonstrations. He represents the revolutionaries who later organized the Sinn Féin movement for independence from

Britain. Although outraged by the Church's denouncement of Parnell on moral grounds, his anger does not make him renounce his faith. He protests he is "no renegade Catholic."

STEPHEN'S WOMEN FRIENDS
Eileen Vance

Eileen Vance, the little girl Stephen wants to marry when he is very young, remains a romantic ideal. As the youngsters frolic together, you see her golden hair streaming in the sun. The feel of her cool white hands like ivory is one of Stephen's earliest sensual experiences. The ivory hands and the golden hair merge into a recurrent phrase, "Tower of Ivory. House of Gold," which is part of the Roman Catholic Litany of Our Lady. Like Stephen's mother, Eileen represents a vision of womanhood associated with the Virgin, but with overtones of warmth and comfort.

Emma (E.C.)

Can you describe Emma? Probably not. She is a provocative look under a hood, dark eyelashes, tapping footsteps, girlish laughter, and not much more. There are few encounters between Stephen and Emma. She may have flirted with a young priest—or she may not have.

Like Mercedes, the heroine of *The Count of Monte Cristo* (by Alexandre Dumas *père*) who nourishes Stephen's fantasy life, or Eileen, Stephen's childhood friend, Emma is a symbol of frustrated romantic fervor. She is there to show you how Stephen relates to women. He is shy, moody. He regrets he didn't take advantage of a chance to kiss her. Instead, he possesses her in his imagination.

Emma's physical image often blends with that of the Blessed Virgin and Church rituals in Stephen's mind. The imagery in the poem (villanelle) he writes about her is both sensuous and religious.

JESUIT MASTERS AT CLONGOWES

Father Dolan

If there is a villain in *Portrait of the Artist*, it is the Clongowes Dean of Studies. He not only hits Stephen harder than necessary, but he also seems to take pleasure in the act and in humiliating him. He is both cruel and unjust. Joyce depicts him vividly as having a "whitegrey" face with "no-colored eyes" behind steel-rimmed eyeglasses. Father Dolan is a central part of the horror of the pandybat incident that is permanently etched in Stephen's memory. His cruelty warns Stephen that all priests are not what they should be. It is the first step toward his later rejection of the Church.

Father Arnall

The Latin teacher is a mild man who tries to be fair. Stephen is surprised to see him angry at times. He concludes that if the priest can permit himself to be angry, anger need not be a sin. But Arnall is also ineffective and weak. He doesn't protect Stephen from the cruelty of Father Dolan, Arnall's superior, and the boy resents this. It is further proof that adults—even priests—as well as boys can be cruel and unfair.

An older, more forceful Arnall turns up later as the retreat master at Belvedere College who strikes terror into Stephen with his lurid sermons on Hell. His warnings of eternal torment for sinners are meant to frighten the boys into conformity.

Father Conmee

The diplomatic rector of Clongowes comforts the indignant Stephen when Stephen complains about the unjust physical punishment inflicted by Father Dolan. But Father Conmee's concern turns out to be hypocritical. Instead of reproaching Father Dolan for his "mistake," Conmee has a good laugh with Dolan about "the manly little chap." The priests once again disappoint Stephen.

CLASSMATES AT BELVEDERE COLLEGE

Vincent Heron

Vincent Heron and Stephen Dedalus, the top students at Belvedere, have a strained relationship. Heron is a tease and a bully. But Stephen and he are constant companions, mainly because both of them feel alienated by their intelligence from other students.

Heron has a bird's face as well as a bird's name. His eagle-like features and his faintly cruel smile call to mind the eagles in the prelude that threaten Stephen's eyes. Heron's repeated, bullying commands that Stephen admit certain things echo the earlier demands that the boy apologize. Like the menacing eagles, Heron is a reminder of social pressure to conform as well as religious pressure to confess one's sins.

Other Classmates

Boland and Nash are ignorant allies of Heron whose attacks on Stephen's literary idols particularly anger him. They help reinforce the image of Stephen as a nonconformist and loner.

DUBLIN UNIVERSITY FRIENDS

Lynch

Lynch is the down-to-earth audience who provides comic relief during Stephen's lengthy, and somewhat overblown, explanation of his artistic conceptions in Chapter Five. Stephen feels contempt for the crass, cynical Lynch, as he does for many of his university classmates. In contrast to Stephen's intellectual and spiritual orientation, Lynch is explicitly, crudely physical; he grimaces, rubs his groin, and admits having eaten dung.

Cranly

Stephen's closest companion Cranly is from a back-country town south of Dublin. In spite of his lack of sophistication and his intellectual inferiority, he plays the role of father confessor to his doubting, religiously tormented friend. Representing the voice of society and tradition in its most understanding form, he tries to warn Stephen of the extreme loneliness he will incur if he leaves Catholicism, Ireland, and the ties of family and friends. His reminders about friendship and love point up Stephen's essential inability to be close to others.

MacCann

The idealistic MacCann represents the liberated Irish intellect of his day. He looks beyond Ireland and works doggedly for world peace. Although, like Stephen, he rejects the narrowness of local concerns, his devotion to abstract ideas of social equality and a united Europe is the opposite of Stephen's solitary devotion to his personal vocation as an artist. In fact, MacCann scolds Stephen for being antisocial and "wrapped up in himself."

Davin

Davin is a simple, rustic student steeped in Irish lore. An ardent nationalist, he tries earnestly to interest Stephen in the Gaelic language of ancient Ireland as well as its present political struggle for independence from England. "A man's country comes first," he tells Stephen. "You can be a poet or mystic after."

Stephen seems fond of Davin and perhaps even envious of the gentle simplicity he knows he lacks himself. He finds himself haunted by Davin's story of a late-night meeting with a mysterious country woman. At the same time however, Davin represents to him an Ireland that by over-romanticizing its past stifles its citizens in the present—the Ireland he must escape.

Other Elements
SETTING

Joyce fled from Dublin to the mainland of Europe, but Dublin never left him. He wrote about the city for the rest of his life— in *Dubliners*, *Portrait of the Artist*, *Ulysses*, and *Finnegans Wake*.

Dublin is more than the backdrop of *Portrait of the Artist*. It is also the symbol of Stephen's discontent. The drab, stagnant city is seen as the heart of a paralyzed Ireland that stifles the aspiring young artist. The city's streets, through which Stephen constantly wanders as he works out his future, are like the labyrinth (maze) constructed by his eponym, the mythical Daedalus. For both of them the only escape is flight.

Stephen's family starts out living in Bray, an affluent seaside village south of Dublin. However, financial problems force the family into the city, first to the suburb of Blackrock, and then to a series of progressively bleaker dwellings in the city's shabbier sections. As you might expect, these downhill moves color Stephen's view of the city and of his life. The Dublin streets reflect his dissatisfaction. There even comes a time when, disgusted with himself, he finds comfort in their foul-smelling filth—they match his own darker moods and self-disgust.

The real Dublin of Joyce's time had its gracious sections adorned by eighteenth-century Georgian brick houses and by many handsome monuments. It also had the natural beauty of Dublin Bay, the outlet of the River Liffey. Stephen is not completely blind to this beauty. In his frequent walks he goes to the water. It is on the harbor's seawall, called the Bull, that he clearly hears the call of his artistic destiny, and on the bay shore that he sees the girl who becomes a symbol of the freedom and beauty he seeks. (Some see the Liffey and the sea as symbols of the "stream" of Stephen's thoughts and as the sites of his rebirth and baptism as an artist.)

But it's the seamy side of Dublin that haunts Stephen in all its sordid detail: water-logged lanes, putrid puddles, dung heaps, odors of fish, "horse piss and rotted straw." Despite any momentary feelings of communion, Stephen must reject the "dull phenomenon of Dublin"—and Ireland—as an environment suitable for artistic growth, even though both city and country will remain a rich source of the art itself.

CATHOLIC IRELAND

Joyce was reared as a Roman Catholic, as were most Irish. In *Portrait of the Artist*, he relives through its hero, Stephen, the struggle to free himself from the Church and its strict control over Irish personal, intellectual, and social life. At the same time, Joyce weaves through Stephen's story religious symbols and imagery, as well as the sense of religious mystery and awe that never left him. Knowing some basic Catholic tenets and rituals will help you understand some of Stephen's conflicts.

The Holy Trinity Roman Catholic dogma affirms the Gospel of Christ as handed down by tradition. Stephen and his classmates learned their catechism—the summary of the principles of the faith—which is based on the existence of the Holy Trinity—Father (God), Son (Jesus Christ), and Holy Ghost (Holy Spirit)—as one.

Mortal Sin To sin is to rebel against God. A sin is mortal if it is both serious and committed deliberately. All Roman Catholics are expected to confess mortal sins, and they are forgiven only if the sinner is truly contrite (remorseful) and repentant (determined to mend his or her ways). The consequences of mortal sin are terrifying. Since the soul of each human being is immortal, one is held responsible after death for actions during life and can be sent for eternity to Heaven or to Hell.

The terrors of the hell that awaits unrepentant sinners are described in vivid detail by Father Arnall in Chapter Three, driving Stephen to seek forgiveness. He confesses his mortal sins—especially his sexual transgressions—and is genuinely contrite at the end of Chapter Three.

Sacraments God's grace—the sign of His own virtues—is given directly through a sacrament to human beings. One of these sacraments—there are seven, including baptism and marriage—is the Eucharist, the sacrament of Communion. In this sacrament, the person who receives Communion partakes of bread—usually a thin wafer—and wine, which turn miraculously into the body and the blood (the substance) of Christ himself. Confession must precede the ritual of Communion and both are required at least once a year at Easter, the celebration of Christ's resurrection. This is the Easter Duty that Stephen refuses in Chapter Five despite his mother's pleas.

Sacrilege   To receive a sacrament without true belief—or under false pretenses, without confession and remorse—is to commit the supreme sin of sacrilege. Even a self-proclaimed nonbeliever like Stephen would hesitate to commit so great an offense. You will see how seriously Stephen takes this potential crime when he talks it over with Cranly in Chapter Five.

Heresy   Roman Catholic policy in Joyce's day condemned fairly large areas of independent philosophical thinking, branding them as heresy because they were deemed to be fundamentally contrary to Catholic beliefs. Stephen is accused of heresy by his English teacher in Chapter Two because a sentence in his essay has strayed in a minor way from accepted theory. This restriction on free thought is another reason Stephen feels compelled to reject the Church.

Jesuits   Joyce, like Stephen, was educated by the Jesuits (members of the order of the Society of Jesus) in three of the most prestigious Jesuit schools in Ireland. Jesuit teachers were, and still are, famous for instilling rigorous standards of intellectual discipline in philosophy and the humanities, as well as in religious matters. There was great intellectual and social prestige, in addition to religious status, in being a Jesuit. You will see that this momentarily tempts Stephen in Chapter Four. Also, Stephen's intellectual orientation and his tendency to dispute things philosophically are considered earmarks of the Jesuit spirit.

IRISH NATIONALISM

Centuries of turbulent, often bloody, history have left their mark on the Ireland of *Portrait of the Artist*, and on Stephen Dedalus. The most troubling issue of that history was Ireland's difficult relations with England.

England, which from the twelfth century had controlled portions of Ireland, gained near-complete dominance of the island in the sixteenth century. Irish resentment of the conquerors was strong, especially when under King Henry VIII the English monarchy became Protestant, while Ireland clung to Roman Catholicism. Irish Catholics became victims of religious persecution in their own country. Unjust agricultural policies also contributed to the difficulties. Most Irish land was owned by absentee landlords and leased to tenant farmers. It was an inefficient system that was in part responsible for a series of Irish famines, the most terrible of which occurred after the failure of the potato crop in 1848. Over a million people died during this famine.

From time to time, revolutionary heroes—like the eighteenth-century patriots Wolfe Tone and Hamilton Rowan admired by young Stephen— aroused Irish hopes for independence, only to be crushed. In Joyce's youth, confrontation was once again in the air. The Land League, led by Michael Davitt and Charles Stewart Parnell, had campaigned successfully for agricultural reforms. Other groups campaigned for Irish cultural independence by promoting the use of Gaelic, Ireland's native tongue, rather than the English brought by Ireland's conquerors. Perhaps most important was the campaign for Irish Home Rule, self-government through an independent Irish parliament.

The Home Rule campaign was led by Charles Stewart Parnell. If your family has ever been divided over a key political issue, you'll understand the vehemence of the argument over the Parnell question when you read the Christmas dinner scene in Chapter One. Parnell's leadership in the British Parliament had succeeded in winning over his colleagues to Home Rule. Before the bill was passed, however, Parnell's enemies exposed his personal relationship with the married Katherine (Kitty) O'Shea, with whom he had been living secretly for many years.

The Parnell affair divided Ireland. Parnell's own party deposed him, the Catholic Church denounced him, and his British backers withdrew their support. Parnell died of pneumonia shortly afterwards, in 1891, when Joyce was nine. (In the infirmary scene in Chapter One, the feverish Stephen dreams of his hero's funeral procession.)

Irish politics remained hopelessly tangled after Parnell's downfall. Some groups still wanted to work for independence by peaceful means. Others believed that violence was necessary. Irish nationalists, like Stephen's friend Davin, joined a group called Sinn Féin, whose military arm was called the Irish Republican Brotherhood (IRB). Remnants of the IRB later became the Irish Republican Army, known as the IRA.

The Sinn Féin's armed Easter Sunday Rebellion of 1916 against the British was unsuccessful in its attempt to seize Dublin and proclaim a republic. The British outlawed the group in 1918 and sent in troops ("Black and Tans") to round up remaining guerrilla fighters. Nevertheless, the Irish Free State (now the Republic of Ireland) was established four years later; it included most, but not all, of Ireland. The six counties of the northern region of Ulster remained, as they are now, a part of Britain—but violently divided over religious issues. Thus, the long tradition of Anglo-Irish conflict continues to this day.

For Stephen, Ireland's history was so unhappy, so bitter, that he wanted nothing to do with it. Let naive idealists like Davin campaign for political and cultural independence. He will have no part of the campaigns. He has seen Ireland destroy too many of her heroes. She is, he says, an old sow that eats her farrow (a pig that eats her young). He can deal with the weight of Irish history not by attempting reform or by revolution—but only by attempting escape.

THE DAEDALUS MYTH

The name Stephen Dedalus was chosen by James Joyce to link his hero with the mythical Greek hero, Daedalus. The Latin epigraph is from the Roman poet Ovid's version of the story.

In Greek myth, Daedalus was an architect, inventor, and craftsman whose name is often translated as "cunning [skillful] artificer." By request of king Minos, Daedalus built a labyrinth—a maze—on Crete to contain a monster called the Minotaur, half bull and half man. Later, for displeasing the king, Daedalus and his son Icarus were both confined in this labyrinth, which was so complex that even its creator couldn't find his way out. Instead, Daedalus fashioned wings of wax and feathers so that he and his son could escape. But when Icarus flew too high—too near the sun—in spite of his father's warnings, his wings melted, and he fell into the sea and drowned. His more cautious father flew to safety.

Joyce had always been drawn to myths—ancient legends and tales that, despite their cultural origins, relate universal themes, like the conflict between father and son or the role of the creative artist. The legend of Daedalus and his headstrong son particularly interested him. He found in it parallels to his own predicament as an artist caught in the maze of his own constricted life, with his own father-son conflict. Like Daedalus, he needed skill and courage to fly away and escape. Joyce signed the name Stephen Daedalus to some of his early stories. Later, when he decided to use the name for the hero of *Portrait of the Artist*, he changed the spelling to Dedalus to make it seem a more Irish last name.

The Daedalus myth gives a basic structure to *Portrait of the Artist*. At first, Stephen doesn't understand the significance of his unusual name. He comes to realize, by the fourth chapter, that like Daedalus he is caught in a maze. If he wants to be free, he must fly high above the obstacles in his path. At the end of Chapter Five, he is poised to try his wings.

The novel echoes the myth on several levels. Stephen seeks a way out of the restraints of family, country, and religion. Like Daedalus, he will fashion his own wings—of poetry, not of wax—as a creative ("cunning") artist. But there are also times when Stephen feels like Icarus, the son who will not heed his father's advice and who died for his stubborn pride. At the end of *Portrait of the Artist*, he seems to be calling on a substitute, spiritual parent for support, when he refers to Daedalus as "old father, old artificer."

The myth's pattern of flight and fall also gives shape to the novel. Some readers see each chapter ending as an attempted flight followed by partial failure—a fall—at the beginning of the next chapter. The last chapter ends with the most ambitious attempt, to fly away from home, religion, and nation to a self-imposed artistic exile. If you identify Joyce with Stephen Dedalus, the last flight will appear to have been a success. As a purely fictional matter, however, it is not certain whether Stephen will soar like Daedalus or drown like Icarus.

THEMES

Many themes are woven into the fabric of *Portrait of the Artist*. Is there one main theme that overrides the others? Readers differ in their views. You may feel, as some do, that the book is chiefly about Stephen's struggle to free himself from his surroundings. It's about his rejection of authority. Or you may see the novel primarily as Stephen's discovery of his artistic vocation. Perhaps you'll agree with those who see in *Portrait of the Artist* mainly the mocking study of a pompous, self-important young egotist.

The following are themes of *Portrait of the Artist*.

1. REJECTION OF AUTHORITY

Stephen's ultimate rebellion is a classic example of a young person's struggle against the conformity demanded of him by society. The young Stephen possesses a childish faith in his family, his religion, and his country. As he matures, he comes to feel these institutions are attempting to destroy his independent spirit. He must escape them to find himself.

Stephen's rebellion is directed against numerous opponents. One is his father, Simon Dedalus. As Stephen discovers that his father is a drunken, ineffectual failure, he rejects his authority.

Stephen also rejects the bonds of a religion that restricts his natural impulses. Catholicism imposes a burden of guilt that weighs him down. He must "admit" and "confess" and "apologise" even when he feels innocent. By rejecting Catholicism, Stephen is also rejecting his devoutly religious mother.

Stephen's rebellion is also directed against his native land. Dirty, backward Ireland destroys any of its children who show creativity; it is, he says, a sow that eats her farrow. His classmates attempt to reform Ireland through political action and promotion of native literature. Stephen rejects these attempts as futile and backward-looking. Instead he abandons Ireland and looks toward the continent.

2. THE DEVELOPMENT OF THE ARTIST

Many readers feel that Stephen's discovery of his artist's calling provides the major framework for the novel. Certainly, from the opening pages of the novel to its end, Joyce emphasizes the boy's sensitive responses to language and to the sights and sounds of the world around him. Words define life: as a schoolboy, he tries to arrange them to see where he fits in the scheme of the universe. He turns to writing poetry to express the emotions he can't express in speech. In time he writes prize essays and even shapes his own theories of beauty.

The desire to be an artist becomes the most powerful force in Stephen's life. You can see three separate—but closely related—aspects of his, and
Joyce's, attitudes toward art.

Art as a vocation or calling   Not everyone who
has an artist's sensitivity chooses art as a vocation.
Stephen ultimately finds that his calling to art is
so strong that he has no choice but to follow it.
Though family, friends, and teachers try to dis-
courage him, he must express himself as freely and
fully as he can, even though the result may be
loneliness, poverty, and exile.

Art as flight   The life of the imagination is a refuge from drab reality for Stephen. But his attempts
to create art are not merely attempts to escape. He
wants not just to reject but to transform. Art will
let him use the negative parts of his world in a
positive way. Art can transform ugliness into
beauty. In the hands of an artist, even the most
foul-smelling Dublin street can become a work
worthy of celebration.

Art as religion   Stephen comes to consider the
pursuit of beauty as a religion. Rejecting the Catholic priesthood, he sees himself as a "priest of the
eternal imagination."

3.   PORTRAIT OF A YOUNG EGOTIST

Some readers feel that the central theme is the
character study of an arrogant, unhappy egotist,
an intensely self-absorbed young man. An egotist
is interested only in the self, and is intensely critical of other people and the world. This can be said
of Stephen, who feels superior and finds it hard
to care for others, even for his own family. It is
equally hard for him to accept affection or love
from others. From his early school days on, he is

at the edge of group life, observing himself. As he grows older, he becomes even more totally absorbed in his own ideas until he finally withdraws from his familiar surroundings. Stephen's opinions on art and his own attempts at writing, as evidenced by the villanelle he writes in Chapter Five, suggest to some that he is not talented enough to justify his self-appointed role as a priest of art.

4. SIN AS A LIBERATING FORCE

In some views, it is Stephen's acceptance of his own sinfulness that sets him free. Guilt and fear of punishment keep him in a sterile, pale world of virtue where he is always hounded by the pressure to confess, admit, or apologize. By committing a mortal (serious) sin of impurity (of the flesh) and falling from grace like Adam from Paradise, or like Lucifer expelled from Heaven, he is thrust back into the earthly world of the senses, a world that releases his creative powers. Stephen will sin again and again, but instead of confessing he will write.

5. LIFE AS A MAZE

From the beginning, Stephen, like most young people, is caught in a maze, just as his namesake Daedalus was. The schools are a maze of corridors; Dublin is a maze of streets. The mind itself is a convoluted maze filled with dead ends and circular reasoning. Life poses riddles at every turn. Stephen roams the labyrinth searching his mind for answers. The only way out seems to be to soar above the narrow confines of the prison, as did Daedalus and his son.

6. PRIDE

Many readers point to Stephen's pride as a cause of his isolation. From the beginning, pride—a mortal sin—keeps him away from others. He yearns for "order and elegance" in his life. He feels superior to his family and to his peers. He feels superior to his country, and to attempts to improve it. In the end, pride drives him to lonely exile. What you must decide is whether Stephen's pride is justified by his talent, or whether it is merely selfish; whether pride has driven him to a fall, as it did Icarus and Lucifer, or whether it will save him.

STYLE

Many readers find Joyce's style one of *Portrait of the Artist*'s greatest strengths. It was Joyce's aim to make his prose "supple [flexible] enough to vary the curve of an emotion," and he shattered tradition to achieve this. He used all the resources of the English language—meaning and sound, as well as structure and spelling—to paint Stephen Dedalus and his world. If you like to read a story told in a traditional way, you may become impatient with Joyce's style. But if you like books, plays, movies, or pictures that *suggest* what things mean instead of telling you directly, you'll enjoy Joyce's world of words.

Joyce is certainly capable of writing in a concrete, realistic manner. The warm, heavy smell of turkey, ham, and celery at Christmas dinner, the clots of liquid dung at the cowyard at Stradbrook—Joyce makes you smell and see these things as richly as does a great realistic writer like Dickens. But for Joyce, language did more than just portray surface reality. It was also linked to an inner world of emotion. Words have shades of meaning and sound

that release feelings below your conscious awareness. For example, the repetition of "white," "cold,"
and "damp," and the images of "fattish white
hands," and a damp cold rat with two "black slimy
eyes" tell you more effectively than long expla-
nations could that Stephen feels very lonely and
anxious as a new boy at school.

Words can also release a chain of thoughts and
memories—the "free association" recommended
in psychoanalysis as a means of revealing innermost concerns. The ugly and suggestive word
"suck" reminds Stephen of the gurgle of dirty water
in a hotel sink. Wine makes him think of both sensual, dark purple grapes and pure white temples.
But it also recalls the sour smell of wine on the
priest's breath on the day of Stephen's first Communion. Joyce developed this idea of free association, in which a character's thoughts are presented as they occur, even if disorganized or
seemingly incoherent, into the interior monologue
or stream-of-consciousness technique. Stephen's
diary at the end of the last chapter is a form of
interior monologue. So are the book's opening
paragraphs, which take you almost directly inside
the mind of a very young child.

Words also have symbolic value. That is, they
can bring to the reader's mind both an immediate,
physical image, and a larger, more abstract con-
cept. Joyce's use of symbolism is more subtle and
complex than that of many other writers. Symbols
in *Portrait of the Artist* usually have more than one
meaning, and their meaning can change as Stephen changes. Some of the symbols you'll encounter most often include the following:

Eyes   From the rhyme, "Pull out his eyes," to

Stephen's loss of his glasses at school, eyes and the loss of vision are associated with fear, vulnerability, and punishment.

Birds and flight Birds can be terrifying and punishing—the eagles that threaten Stephen's eyes, and Stephen's hostile friend Heron. But increasingly they become symbols of freedom and creativity—the hawk-like man, Daedalus, the girl by the water who reminds Stephen of a seabird.

Roses In general, Joyce uses roses to symbolize beauty, art, and women. Their meaning can change with their color. Stephen's musings about a green rose seem to represent his desire to be an artist—to create something, like a green rose, that doesn't exist in nature. White roses are linked to purity.

Water and the sea Especially early in the book, water—the water in the "ditch," the dirty water Stephen thinks of when he hears the word "suck"—is an unpleasant image, linked to urine, filth, and a dirty sexuality. Later, however, water and the sea come to stand for creation—for life, death, and rebirth. As Stephen looks out to sea at the end of Chapter Four, he understands that the sea is both an element in which a person can drown—like Icarus—and a symbol of renewed life. The repeated sea images seem to suggest that Stephen has been reborn as an artist and is undergoing baptism.

Colors also have symbolic value that can change from situation to situation. Joyce uses "white" to show both purity and sickliness. Green suggests healthy lushness but also decay. Yellow is almost always used to portray squalor and ugliness, and rose-pink usually indicates romance.

Where traditional words or combinations of words

won't achieve the desired effect, Joyce brilliantly violates the rules. He breaks down the barriers between the senses in unusual pairings of words—the "smell of evening" or the "soft grey silence." He fuses adjectives and nouns together to create words like "jeweleyed," "cellardamp," and "roselight" that strike the eye with greater impact. Because he felt quotation marks were ugly, he replaced them with dashes. Joyce also liked having fun with language. He played with the "wayward rhythms" of words. "Ivy" and "white" spin off into ivy that whines and twines, then turn into ivory ivy, and end up suggesting an elephant with an ivory tusk.

You'll notice, too, how the style of *Portrait of the Artist* changes with Stephen's age. The first chapter is written in the simple, choppy sentences of a toddler. ("It made him very tired to think that way. It made him feel his head very big.") The language develops and becomes more elaborate as Stephen matures. It also fluctuates with Stephen's mood. It's spare and logical when Stephen discusses ideas, rich and lyrical when he describes emotions. In fact, it becomes so rich and lyrical that some readers suspect Joyce is poking fun at a young man who loves language but doesn't always use it wisely. It's a mistake that Joyce himself seldom made.

POINT OF VIEW

Just as the literary style of *Portrait of the Artist* is more subtle and in some ways more difficult than that of traditional novels, so is the novel's point of view. *Portrait of the Artist* is, in general, an example of a third-person, limited omniscient narrative. Stephen Dedalus doesn't tell his story himself. But in general you perceive only what he perceives. You don't enter other characters' minds. Only occasionally—as at the Christmas dinner scene, or during the trip to Cork with Simon Dedalus—do you even hear or see other characters who haven't been completely filtered through Stephen's perceptions. Indeed, the book focuses so closely on Stephen, and takes you so deeply into his mind, that at times it resembles a first-person narrative.

In fact, however, the book is a little more tricky than that. If *Portrait of the Artist* were a first-person narrative, or a traditional third-person, limited omniscient narrative, it would be difficult for you to get outside of Stephen. You would see him only as he sees himself. You could judge him only as he judges himself. But that isn't what happens.

First, Joyce very occasionally lets you step outside of Stephen's consciousness. For example, at the end of the Christmas dinner scene, you're told that Stephen raises "his terrorstricken face." Stephen, of course, can't see his own face while sitting at the dinner table—but by taking you outside Stephen for this instant, Joyce emphasizes the impact the vicious argument has had upon the young boy.

More subtly, and more frequently, Joyce lets you stand just slightly outside Stephen—in this way giving you the distance you need to judge him—through the language he uses to describe Stephen's thoughts. For example, in Chapter Two, Stephen dreams of finding "in the real world the unsubstantial image which his soul so constantly beheld. . . . They would meet quietly as if they had known each other and had made their tryst . . . and at that moment of supreme tenderness he would be transfigured." Some readers feel such sentences are merely accurate descriptions of Stephen's thoughts; they feel that since Stephen approves of his own thoughts, Joyce does too. But many other readers feel that Joyce has purposely laid it on a little too thick here, and in many other parts of the book. They feel the language he uses to express Stephen's thoughts is purposely a little *too* "poetic," because Stephen himself is a little too poetic. He takes himself, his art, and his rebellion too seriously. Even the famous lines—"Welcome, O life! I go to encounter for the millionth time the reality of experience and to forge in the smithy of my soul the uncreated conscience of my race"—can be taken as a brave vow or as an eloquent-sounding but hollow promise that Stephen won't be able to fulfill.

In these ways, language in *Portrait of the Artist* becomes closely connected to point of view. You are inside Stephen's mind, yet Joyce's language may put you slightly outside it as well. As you read *Portrait of the Artist*, you'll have to decide for yourself what you think of Stephen Dedalus—and then decide how Joyce's language and point of view have led you to make your judgment.

FORM AND STRUCTURE

Portrait of the Artist is divided into five chapters, each composed of episodes. Most episodes are separated by asterisks. The scenes go back and forth in time without alerting the reader to the transition. They represent clusters of meaningful periods in Stephen Dedalus' life.

How does this collection of episodes add up to a unified whole? Some see the basic framework of *Portrait of the Artist* as a five-chapter, chronological progression from small boy to university student. According to this view, each of the five chapters represents a stage in the growth of Stephen's character: his childhood, the shift from childhood to adolescence, the discovery of his true vocation as a writer, and his final decision to be an artist-in-exile. The discovery of his literary vocation provides the book's climax, and his decision to go abroad its resolution—a pattern like that of a musical symphony or a classical Greek drama.

Other readers see *Portrait of the Artist* as having a three-part structure that reflects the three crucial periods of Stephen's self-awareness. The first two chapters concern Stephen's awakening to his own body. The next two show his developing awareness that he must be a writer (and not a priest). The fifth chapter focuses on his realization that he must leave Ireland.

Yet another view concentrates on the rhythmic movement of each chapter from a low point of self-doubt to a moment of triumph. The action rises slowly, only to fall at the beginning of the next chapter. It's a pattern that's been compared to a series of waves. It has also been linked to the myth that underlies the novel—the myth of Daedalus. Each chapter can be seen as an attempted flight. At the chapter's end, Stephen soars. But at the opening of the following chapter, he is brought down to earth once again. At the book's end, Stephen is ready to make his most daring test of his wings. Whether he will succeed like Daedalus, or fall and drown like Daedalus' too-proud son, Icarus, is left for the future.

Still others read the book's basic pattern as an analogy to the birth process. In the first chapter, the embryo is barely formed. Later, the embryo develops a heart, its sex is defined, and it finds it must leave the mother's womb to breathe the outside air. The final chapter leads up to the actual moment of birth and departure from the womb of family, religion, and country.

To further unify this novel, Joyce uses special literary devices that take the place of transitions and plot developments. One is the myth of Daedalus that underlies the novel. (See the section on the Daedalus myth.) Linked to it is another myth, that of Lucifer (Satan), the fallen angel who, out of pride, refuses to serve God.

Figures of speech—images and symbols—also help to flesh out the bare bones of the story, and to suggest tone and mood. They become a vital part of the structure, extended motifs that wind in and out of the story to lead you through the maze of Stephen's experience. (See the section on Style.)

The use of recurrent words and references to create a structure was part of Joyce's pioneer effort to express a deeper reality than that expressed by conventional narratives. Your understanding of the structure depends much on your ability to pick out and interpret the connecting material.

The Story

A Portrait of the Artist as a Young Man asks much of you as a reader. It seems at first like an unrelated medley of sketches, snatches of dialogue, and fragments of action, thought, and feelings. But you'll find, as you continue, that these are related in Stephen's mind. With careful reading they will come together like the pieces of a puzzle to form a "portrait" of Stephen Dedalus, a young man who is developing into an artist.

Each of the five chapters represents a crucial period of Stephen's self-understanding, and is composed of scenes that don't follow each other in obvious order. Joyce separates these scenes (except in Chapter Five) with asterisks. For easier understanding, this guide has inserted headings where these asterisks occur. Headings have also been added at the beginning of each chapter and in Chapter Five, which has no asterisks.

CHAPTER ONE

The first chapter has four parts, including a prelude. Each part is a different scene from Stephen's early childhood.

Prelude
This brief prologue may seem at first a random jumble of childish memories. But you'll find that every word counts. Joyce always prided himself on including most of his main themes in his opening sections, and he has done that in *Portrait of the Artist*. Watch for hidden meanings and clues to themes and motifs you'll find again later.

A small boy, Stephen, is awakening to life. His earliest memories are fragmentary and reflect the language of infancy and early childhood. His first one is of his father telling him a story about a "moocow" coming down the road. The "hairy" father is looking down at his son, "baby tuckoo," through a glass. Stephen also remembers singing a song about a rose.

NOTE: The father's "glass" is probably a monocle, although some think it may be a stein of beer, because Stephen's (and Joyce's) father is a heavy drinker. The "hairy" (bearded) father is thought to be a symbol of God, since father and God are both authority figures for the little boy. The moo-cow—symbol of Ireland—refers to a traditional Irish tale of a white cow that takes children to an island kingdom to train them as heroes. You'll see cows again later. The rose is an important symbol of love and beauty that recurs throughout *Portrait of the Artist*.

Stephen next recalls some childish sense impressions. All five senses are represented: the feel of the wetness of his bed, the smell of the oilsheet (waterproof sheet), the sound of music, the taste of lemon-flavored candy, the sight of his governess Dante's maroon and green brushes. The clarity and creativity of his perceptions already suggest an artistic sensitivity.

Now there is a serious crisis in the tot's world. He seems to have done something that angered the grownups. He must apologize or the eagles will pull out his eyes, says Dante. He turns the frightening words into a rhythmic rhyme: "Apologise,/Pull out his eyes." The threat of punishment for his sins recurs frequently in *Portrait of the Artist* in similar forms. Stephen will be asked again and again to "admit," "confess," or "submit"—grownup versions of the earlier "apologise." The toddler is already struggling with guilt. The threat of blindness, too, is one that will recur. Birds like the eagle will also reappear—both as threatening symbols and as symbols of creativity and freedom.

NOTE: What has Stephen done for which he must atone? Why does he hide under the table? It probably has something to do with Eileen, the little girl he plans to marry. Is it a parallel situation to one in Joyce's early life? Scholars have determined that Joyce and a girl named Eileen Vance were close friends as children. The family's governess, Dante Conway (the Dante Riordan of the novel), did warn Joyce that he would go to Hell if he married Eileen, who was a Protestant.

Brief as it is, this prelude tells you a good deal. You meet some of Stephen's family and friends, whom you'll know far better before the first chapter ends. You see some of Joyce's favorite symbols, like the rose, eyes, and flying (eagles).

You are also introduced to some of the key themes to be developed later: the struggle against conformity, the revolt against parental authority, the lure of sex (Stephen is already drawn to Eileen), the political problems of Ireland (Dante's maroon and green hair-brushes are symbols of political issues: the maroon brush stands for Michael Davitt, the green brush for Charles Stewart Parnell, both Irish nationalist leaders), and the sensitive artistic personality.

The prelude combines the language and subject matter of a small boy's mind so that you see things as he does, as if you were part of the story.

NOTE: Music had a great influence on Joyce. Both he and his father had fine voices. Joyce once seriously considered becoming a professional singer. Here, little Stephen sings a song—"his song"— and dances to a tune. Joyce used his musical talent, not on the stage, but in his writing, where the

sound of words is often as important as their
meaning and even adds to their meaning.

The three episodes that follow present Stephen
as a young child at Clongowes (its full name is
Clongowes Wood College), a Catholic boarding
school run by the Jesuit order, at home in Bray for
the Christmas holidays, and back again at school.

Stephen's years at Clongowes correspond with
Joyce's own stay there between the ages of six and
nine. Stephen is probably six in the opening Clongowes episode. Joyce bares a cross section of the
little boy's mind as it darts back and forth between
memories of home and his first school experiences.

First School Experience
From Stephen's earliest memories in the prelude,
the story shifts abruptly to a schoolyard at Clongowes. Boys are in the midst of a rough-and-tum-
ble ball game. Stephen is afraid and only pretends
to be playing, just to keep out of trouble. He is
clearly not one of the boys; he feels small, weak,
and inadequate. The words "small" and "weak"
are sprinkled throughout this section.

The overall feeling in this section is one of isolation and homesickness. The section also hints at
some themes that will be explored more fully later.
Nasty Roche asks Stephen, "What kind of name
is Dedalus?" Stephen doesn't answer—but eventually he'll see the importance of his name. To
Roche's next question, Stephen replies that his
father is "a gentleman." But unlike the fathers of
some other boys, Stephen's father isn't a "magis-
trate" (a judge). This is Joyce's way of revealing
that although for the time being Simon Dedalus

can afford to send his son to an expensive school, his income and his social position are precarious compared to those of the other fathers. You'll soon see how precarious they are.

One of the most unpleasant things to happen to Stephen at school is his being pushed by another boy, Wells, into a cold and slimy cesspool, the "square ditch."

NOTE: There was a student named Wells at Clongowes in Joyce's time, and he may have been the boy who pushed young James Joyce into the square ditch. Joyce also uses the real names of other students, including Nasty Roche. If you were writing a novel, would you use the names of actual people? Why?

As Stephen thinks about his time at school, he also thinks about the words he's learned there. His growing appreciation for language becomes one of the most important themes in the book. A "belt" can be worn around a suit. It can also be a hit, a punch. (This is a simple example of the puns that Joyce loved in writing.) A page or so later, Stephen broods about the word "suck." Its sound is ugly, and it evokes two separate, unpleasant images— Simon Moonan, a teacher's pet, flattering the priest, and the sound of dirty water running down a drain. (You'll see that water almost always has unpleasant associations in the first part of the book.) Stephen's interest in language will grow, and will be a factor in his decision to become a writer.

In arithmetic class, Stephen, a good student, has been made head of York, the "white rose" team, which is pitted, as always, against Lancaster, the "red rose" team. Stephen tries hard, but the red rose team wins.

NOTE: Significance of the rose   The names of the arithmetic teams refer to the names of the opposing forces in fifteenth-century England's Wars of the Roses. The House of Lancaster had been represented by the red rose; the House of York by the white rose. Ireland enlisted under the banner of York, which lost the war. As a result of these dynastic conflicts, Henry VII, founder of the Tudor dynasty, became king and began to replace the Irish nobility with English lords, a policy that was a major source of conflict between the two countries. Thus, by being captain of the white rose team, Stephen champions Ireland against England. Later, you'll see that he does resent England for imposing its culture and language on his country. However, you'll also see that he can't identify with Ireland either.

Other roses crop up frequently in *Portrait of the Artist*. The wild rose is part of the toddler's earliest memories in the prelude. The rose has many associations for Stephen. It is linked with women, love, and beauty, including the beauty of art.

The boy observes that the Jesuit master in charge of the math class, Father Arnall, seems cross but is really chuckling. This is one of the many times Stephen will notice the hypocrisy of the priests, as his doubts about religion develop. In Clongowes, Arnall is shown as a reasonably fair teacher. Later on, as retreat master at Belvedere College, he will play a darker role in Stephen's religious life.

Wells, who knocked Stephen into the square ditch, now harasses him with a question—"Do you kiss your mother before you go to bed?" No matter how Stephen answers, he's laughed at. The question is linked in his mind with other questions: about sexuality (why do people kiss?), about God and the universe, thoughts so complex they make him tired.

Stephen begins to feel sick and feverish. Perhaps his tumble into the ditch has made him ill. He prays, and dreams of going home to his family. On awakening he discovers he is indeed ill and is sent to the infirmary. A fellow student, Athy, comments again on Stephen's unusual last name and asks him more riddles. At this point much of life is a riddle to Stephen. Perhaps the chief one is his father. Who is he? What is his role in the world? Understanding his father is an important part of Stephen's understanding of himself.

NOTE: The Daedalus myth   Once again, Joyce brings up the question of Stephen's last name. At this point, Stephen doesn't grasp the meaning of "Dedalus." Later, he'll come to understand that he shares his name with Daedalus, the inventor of ancient Greek myth who constructed an imprisoning maze and then had to create a means of escape from it. Can you already see how this story might relate to Stephen? (See the section on the Daedalus myth.)

While Stephen is ill, the news of the nationalist

leader Parnell's death weaves itself into a dream. In the dream Dante, Stephen's governess, is one of the chief mourners. She's draped in maroon for Davitt, green for Parnell. (In fact you saw a few pages earlier that Dante removed the green backing from her hair brush because Parnell was now "a bad man.") Parnell's death, and its consequences for Irish politics and for Stephen's family, will be dramatized further in the next section of the chapter.

NOTE: As you look back on this section, note how Joyce consistently uses repeated details of color, lightness and darkness, sounds, and other sense impressions to convey Stephen's frame of mind. Images like wetness, coldness, and whiteness provide the links that connect fragments of his memory. In the bleak playground scene, the colors convey coldness; the light is gray, Stephen's suit is gray, his cold hands are blue. When he is feeling ill, the word "white" is repeated frequently to suggest both a hospital environment and Stephen's pale, youthful virtue, or purity. As you read, try to find other sensory words that Joyce uses to convey emotional messages.

The Christmas Dinner

Joyce's portrayal of a Christmas dinner ruined by an argument is one of the most famous scenes in *Portrait of the Artist*. Because Joyce uses the dinner primarily to reveal the characters and issues that surround his hero, it's one of the few scenes in the book whose action isn't fully filtered through Stephen's consciousness. Instead, it's presented to you directly, as it would be in a more conventional novel or in a play. As a result, the scene has great dramatic tension. It's also very funny—Joyce shows you the bitterness that can divide a household, but he also shows you the humor contained in that bitterness, as adults behave like children throwing tantrums over their political differences.

The dinner episode marks the beginning of Stephen's loss of faith in religion, because the Church seems responsible for destroying the great political hero, Parnell. It's also a compact summary, in dramatic terms, of the political turmoil that divided many Irish families after Parnell's disgrace and death.

The bright Christmas setting of the Dedalus living room is in abrupt contrast to Stephen's gloomy school experiences. It's the first time Stephen is old enough to join the grownups at the Christmas table. You'll see that this dinner is a turning point for the little boy in more ways than one.

NOTE: This is the last time Stephen's family is portrayed as well off. Like Joyce's own family, the Dedalus clan is in for hard times. Tonight there is turkey and ham and a "big plum pudding." By the final chapter, Stephen is drinking watery tea and dipping crusts of fried bread into "yellow drippings" of fat usually from cooked bacon or pork.

The conversation around the table soon turns into an unpleasant political argument between Dante and a family friend, Mr. John Casey. Simon Dedalus, Stephen's father, joins in. The quarrel centers on Charles Stewart Parnell, whose funeral had entered Stephen's dream in the previous section. Parnell had been denounced by the Catholic Church because of his long-time affair with the married Kitty O'Shea. The scandal led to his fall from political power and perhaps contributed to his death. With him fell Ireland's chances for obtaining Home Rule.

NOTE: As you observe this bitter argument, ask yourself which side you think Stephen supports. You'll be told in the next chapter. Joyce himself was strongly pro-Parnell as a boy. When he was nine years old, he wrote a poem attacking one of his hero's foes.

John Casey and Simon Dedalus condemn the Church for attacking Parnell. They insist the Church should not "preach politics from the altar." But Dante has deserted her former hero to side with her faith. "God and religion before everything!" she cries. She prophesies that Stephen will long remember this bitter attack against religion in his own home. Mr. Dedalus retorts that what the boy will remember is the guilt of the priests who drove Parnell to his grave. As you'll see, both prophecies will be fulfilled.

The heat of the argument terrifies Stephen. It has brought out startling flaws in the adults he admired. The smiling Casey is capable of rage, and can do something as crude as spit tobacco juice into the eyes of an old woman. Stephen's father becomes coarse and bestial in his language, and the usually restrained Dante loses control and almost spits in Casey's face. As a result, Stephen's sense of insecurity deepens. The quarrel has given him cause to doubt his family circle, the Church, and a country that turns against its hero for incomprehensible reasons.

Some readers point out that the Christmas dinner scene is a good example of what Joyce called an epiphany—a special, sudden moment of truth. Although the dinner argument focuses on politics, its meaning for Stephen is much deeper. It causes him to doubt the institutions and people he has been told to believe in. Those doubts will grow.

NOTE: The motif of eyes and blindness is woven through this scene as it was earlier. The old woman who shouts that she is blinded is one example. Can you find others in this sequence? Being blind is of course a symbol for not understanding the world or oneself clearly; in *Portrait of the Artist*, blindness or the threat of it usually comes as a punishment.

Joyce's poor eyesight was always on his mind. It plagued him early in life and steadily deteriorated. He was nearly blind in his mature years in spite of a series of operations. His faulty vision may have contributed to his strong musical sensitivity and keen ear for the sounds of language. Joyce studied languages at university, and also taught himself (and others).

The Pandybat Scene
Back at Clongowes, Stephen is faced with the realities of authority, guilt, and punishment. There has been a school scandal. Some boys who ran away have been caught and will either be publicly flogged or expelled.

Stephen is not sure what the runaways are guilty of. Some boys say that they stole money from the rector's (headmaster's) room. Others think they stole wine used for communion. Athy, Stephen's companion in the infirmary, insists he knows: the boys were indulging in "smugging" (schoolboy homosexual acts) with younger boys in the lavatory.

The rumors revive the veiled sexual connotations of the first scene at Clongowes. Stephen doesn't know what smugging is or why the boys chose to do it in the dank, unpleasant lavatory. The offense must be serious, because the punishment is severe. Joyce again emphasizes Stephen's state of sexual innocence (purity) at this stage of his life.

NOTE: One of the graffiti written on the toilet walls is "The Calico Belly," a gross schoolboy pun on the Latin title of Julius Caesar's famous treatise on his Gallic wars, *Commentarii de Bello Gallico*. Even the youngest pupils at Clongowes studied Latin, and Caesar's work was standard early reading.

One of the boys involved in the scandal is nicknamed Lady Boyle, because he has a delicate air and is always paring his fingernails. Boyle's hands remind Stephen of the slender white hands of Eileen, the little playmate he wants to marry in the prelude. He recalls an innocent sensual moment when she placed her soft, cool hand in his pocket and touched his own.

NOTE: Eileen's streaming golden hair and her cool white hands make Stephen think of the phrases

"Tower of Ivory" and "House of Gold," part of a
prayer to the Virgin Mary. This is one of the many
times throughout the book that the young boy's
erotic feelings are linked to images of the Virgin.
The hands of Boyle and Eileen are clearly related
to sexual awakening, but their whiteness suggests
that the sexuality is still pure and basically dor-
mant. The whiteness is connected to the ivory tower
of the Virgin, another image of combined sensuality and innocence.

Stephen and his classmates fear that because of
the smuggling scandal, a general punishment will
be meted out to the whole student body. They
particularly dread pandying, the striking of the
palms with a pandybat, a leather strap stiffened
with whale bone.

In the classroom, Father Arnall has excused Stephen from work because his eyeglasses have been
smashed. But Father Dolan, the rector's assistant,
punishes him with the dreaded pandybat for not
writing. He insists Stephen is merely pretending
his glasses are broken so he can avoid studying.
The "firm soft fingers" of the priest steady Stephen's hands for the punishment as the pandybat
descends on Stephen's palms.

NOTE: Joyce himself was unfairly pandied by a
Father James Daly while he was at Clongowes, and
for the same unjust reason. Stephen's reactions to
the pandying are clearly autobiographical. Stephen mentions two more pandyings later in the
book, saying he had deserved more. Records in
the punishment book at Clongowes show at least

three more pandyings for Joyce: one for forgetting to bring a book to class, one for wearing muddy boots in the house, and one for "vulgar language."

You'll notice, too, how threatened blindness (Stephen's loss of his glasses) is linked to punishment.

Added to Stephen's physical pain is the humiliation of having to kneel in the middle of the classroom. But most dreadful of all, as you know if you have ever been unjustly punished, is realizing that life often is unjust. The phrase that occurs throughout this section is "cruel and unfair."

In view of the fact that he had been excused from writing, Stephen particularly resents Father Arnall's lukewarm defense. Even priests can be cruel and unfair. Again, Stephen's faith in the authority of his elders is shaken as it was at the Christmas dinner. His disappointment with the priests (false fathers) in his educational environment will be no less than his disappointment with his own father.

Stephen's classmates encourage him to complain to the rector, Father Conmee. Heartened by the example of great men of valor he has read about, he sets off on the long, difficult journey to the rector's office.

Note the way Joyce chooses details to set the mood of Stephen's sense of doom. The office is hushed. There is a skull on the desk (a reminder of man's ultimate fate?) and a "strange solemn smell in the room." Stephen trembles as he tells his story. But the rector is kindly. He soothes the shaky lad and assures him he will straighten out Father Dolan's "mistake."

Stephen, feeling victorious, races back down the path he had followed so hesitantly before. His schoolmates cheer him as a conquering hero. Justice is triumphant—at least for the moment. Not only has he won over the dark forces of unjust priests, but he has overcome his own fear. It is a turning point: "He was happy and free."

In this moment of victory, however, Stephen tries to remember not to gloat or give in to pride, but to remain modest and obedient. For now, his triumph as a rebel, the climax of this chapter, results in a resolve to conform. But the battle between rebellion and conformity, between pride and obedience, will continue throughout *Portrait of the Artist*, and its future outcome may be different.

CHAPTER TWO

The five scenes of this chapter span some five or six years. Stephen was nine at the end of Chapter One and will be about fourteen at the end of Chapter Two. Joyce leaves it to you to figure out the time gaps between scenes.

The victorious little boy of the last chapter has new troubles. As his family slides down the social scale because of money problems, Stephen makes a painful transition from childhood to adolescence. Joyce selects incidents that contrast Stephen's outward conformity with his inner turmoil. Stephen lives in romantic daydreams that mask sexual urges he barely understands. By the end of the chapter, he has come to terms with his physical self; he has found sexual release. You may see this as a new victory, as Stephen does. Or will the new freedom lead to his downfall?

Blackrock
The Dedalus family has moved to Blackrock, a suburb some eight miles from Dublin. There, Stephen
spends much of the summer with his great uncle
Charles. Every Sunday he walks with Charles and
his father, who talk of Irish politics, sports, and
family lore. On week days, Uncle Charles and his
old friend, Mike Flynn, a former track coach, su-
pervise Stephen's running practice. Stephen also
spends time riding in a milk truck and roaming
the Irish countryside with a gang of boys.

This is the leisurely old Ireland that will try—
unsuccessfully—to claim Stephen. Eventually he
will reject it completely as stagnant and stifling.
But for now his attitude is more confused. On the
one hand, he enjoys running errands with Uncle
Charles. On the other hand, Mike Flynn with his
lusterless blue eyes is an object of pity. Soon Flynn
will be hospitalized, and Uncle Charles will slip
into senility—symbols of old Ireland's decline.

In the same way, Stephen has mixed feelings
about his peers. With the gang of boys he's joined
he enjoys typical boyish pleasures—sneaking into
gardens, fighting mock battles. But if on the surface Stephen seems much like the other boys, un-
derneath he feels separated from them. He longs
to be part of the real world around him but doesn't
quite know how to do this. Often he retreats into
fantasies that are nourished by Alexandre Dumas'
romantic tale, *The Count of Monte Cristo*. Its heroine, Mercedes, is now the focus of his idealized
and surpressed sexuality, just as Eileen Vance was
earlier. He imagines Mercedes in a white house,
bright with rosebushes. As with Eileen and the
Virgin, the color white indicates the spiritual side

of these fantasies. And the roses are a recurrent reminder of beauty and romance.

As autumn approaches, life, like nature, takes on a darker hue. Stephen will not return to Clongowes. His father can't afford the school: the hints you've seen earlier about Simon Dedalus' precarious finances are being proved accurate. As Stephen observes the countryside, the pastoral scenes that only a few weeks before delighted him now seem oppressive. Notice how Joyce employs cows (which, you'll remember from the "moocows" in the book's opening, are a symbol of Ireland) to show Stephen's growing discontent. In the summer, the cows in their pasture had seemed beautiful to him. Now it's autumn, and they've been brought back to a filthy cowyard that with its "foul green puddles and clots of liquid dung" sickens Stephen's heart. It's a clear sign that Stephen's affection for his native land is waning.

Stephen's vague unrest deepens as he broods over the fictional Mercedes and longs to find a real girl just like her. Like many an adolescent, he dreams of a magic moment of "supreme tenderness" in which he will shed his timidity and turn into a strong, fearless man. To relieve his restlessness, he wanders alone. The motif of solitary walking to work out troubling problems will be repeated many times.

Joyce is accused of writing "purple" prose—overemotional writing—in passages like those that describe Stephen's adolescent longings. Do you think they are overdone, or are they true to the way a youth imbued with romantic literature would express his feelings? Do you think Joyce is making fun of this side of Stephen? Many find in this scene an example of the irony that the narrator employs to distance himself from Stephen and be critical of him.

Move to Dublin
Large yellow vans move Stephen's family one morning to a cheerless house right in Dublin. His mother weeps, and his father blames nameless "enemies" for his financial problems. But the boy senses that the forced move is his father's fault. He is losing faith in him.

NOTE: The color yellow is often used by Joyce to denote ugliness, disgust, and depression. Watch for mention of "thick yellow scum," "yellow dripping," yellow lamps, and other yellows in this chapter and later ones.

Stephen finds Dublin gloomy, foggy, and squalid. He feels embittered. It's increasingly hard for him to relate to other people or to accept affection. If you, like many readers, believe that Stephen is at least in part a self-centered young egotist, you can see that side of him developing here, as he grows "angry . . . with the change of fortune which was reshaping the world about him into a vision of squalor and insincerity."

During a visit, an aged relative mistakes Stephen for a girl, "Josephine." It's an incident that may imply that along with his other problems Stephen is suffering adolescent doubts about his sexuality. It echoes the smugging episode in the first chapter. There will be similar echoes in the next scene.

At a party where Stephen feels more than ever an outsider, the come-hither glance of a young girl attracts him. The pair take the last tram (streetcar) home together. Stephen feels that the girl, referred to as E.C., is inviting a kiss, but he lets the opportunity pass. Later, devoured by regret, he tries to pour out his feelings in a poem where he does kiss her. The budding poet finds it easier to write than to act; you'll see the same pattern in Chapter Five, when Stephen writes another poem, a villanelle. (Notice, too, that he's already made one attempt at writing a poem, in praise of Parnell. Now you know whom he supported in the argument at Christmas dinner.)

NOTE: Stephen's women The girl Stephen rides with on the streetcar is a dimly seen figure whom Joyce describes only by the expression in her eyes. In *Stephen Hero*, she was more fully drawn. There she was called Emma Clery. Here she is merely called Emma or E.C.

Emma may have been inspired in part by Joyce's intense feelings for Mary Sheehy, one of the six children of the Sheehy family whom he visited every Sunday during his last two years at Belvedere College, the school he attended after Clongowes.

Whether he calls the girl Eileen, Emma, or Mercedes, Stephen is evoking the eternal, desired—and often virginal—female. He links her with sexually inaccessible figures like the Virgin and his own mother.

Stephen hasn't been going to school. Simon Dedalus can no longer afford Clongowes; the alternative he can afford, the Christian Brothers' school, he condemns as being only good enough for "Paddy

Stink and Mickey Mud"—his disparaging terms for the lower middle-class Irish. Only the Jesuits—rich, well-fed, and able to land Stephen a good job after graduation—will do. What does this discussion of schools tell you, and Stephen, about Simon Dedalus?

Simon chances to meet Father Conmee, the former rector of Clongowes, who has left the school to take a higher post in the Jesuit order. Conmee makes it possible for Stephen and his brother Maurice to attend Belvedere College as "free boys," scholarship students.

NOTE: Joyce himself did attend the scorned Christian Brothers' school for some months. Then he and his brother Stanislaus (Maurice in *Portrait of the Artist*) transferred to Belvedere College, a Jesuit day school for middle-class Dublin boys who couldn't afford boarding school. It was less fashionable than Clongowes, but it provided a thorough education.

The encounter with Father Conmee has great impact on Stephen in an unexpected way. Simon reports untactfully at the dinner table that Conmee and Father Dolan had "a great laugh" over Stephen's complaint about the pandying. He also praises Dolan's diplomacy in receiving the boy's protest with humor. In retelling this incident, Stephen's father shatters his son's illusions about his moment of triumph. Joyce only reports the scene; he doesn't take you inside Stephen's mind to analyze it. But how do you think Stephen now feels about himself? the priests? his father? Should Simon Dedalus have repeated the conversation to Stephen? Do you think he takes pleasure in cutting down his young son?

This brief episode is another example of an epiphany, a moment of revelation that, like a beam of light, illuminates a hidden truth.

The Whitsuntide Play

Stephen is now at the end of his second year at Belvedere. It is a difficult time for him. On the one hand, he has made his mark as a scholar. On the other, he is still an outsider, mocked by his peers for being "a model youth."

If you look beneath Stephen's "quiet obedience," there is turmoil. He is angry, insecure, and mistrusts the world. He feels both superior to and alienated from his classmates. His father embarrasses him, while Dublin's dullness depresses him. To rise above reality, he reshapes it in his imagination—the theme of art as creative flight. Do you think this is creativity or only escapism, a common trait of adolescence?

Stephen has a leading part in the annual Whitsuntide school play. (Whitsuntide is the British name for the Pentecost, a Christian church holiday that occurs six weeks after Easter. In England and Ireland, it also marks a school vacation period.) Yet in the midst of the hustle and bustle, he feels impatient and uneasy. He hopes the girl he likes will be in the audience. A little boy has been made up as a girl for the play. This irritates Stephen. Why does it make him so uncomfortable? Some link this incident to the earlier scene in which Stephen is mistaken for a girl. These incidents suggest that

Stephen is unsure of his own sexual identity, of his own as yet unproven manhood.

Stephen's chief scholastic rival, Vincent Heron, teases him about the "deucedly pretty girl" who is coming to the play. Heron strikes Stephen's leg playfully with the cane he sports, and urges him to "admit" he's no saint. Stephen pretends to recite the Confiteor, a ritual prayer of confession. The command "Admit!" repeated twice reminds him of an earlier, painful incident with Heron.

Joyce makes sure you'll notice Heron's symbolic bird's name by giving him birdlike features as well—a beaked face and hair like a crest. He pecks at Stephen like a bird of prey, a reminder of the threatening eye-plucking eagles of the prelude.

In a flashback, Stephen recalls that his English teacher had accused him—half in jest—of making a heretical statement in one of his weekly essays. It is clear that Stephen had been reading authors whose beliefs are deemed contrary to Catholic teachings. (See the section on Catholic Ireland.) After class, Heron and two of his bullying friends had confronted Stephen. They insisted he "admit" that one of his favorite authors, the nineteenth-century Romantic poet Lord Byron, was a heretic, "no good," and immoral. But Stephen refused to be untrue to his intellectual beliefs even though the boys had physically attacked him. He had torn himself away without "admitting."

In both the incidents with Heron, you can see the pressures of conformity through guilt. You can also see the evidence of Stephen's stubborn (and lonely) independence. Joyce also probably means you to see Stephen as a martyr, like his Christian namesake, St. Stephen, the first Christian martyr, who was stoned to death in A.D. 34.

NOTE: Lord Byron was known for his free-thinking and reputedly licentious ways, as well as for his intensely emotional poetry. He was the free spirit—and poet—that Stephen would like to be. On the other hand, the nineteenth-century Catholic philosopher Cardinal John Henry Newman—another of Stephen's literary models—is safe from religious attack. He wrote with restrained and dignified eloquence. He was also one of the founders of University College, which Stephen will later attend.

As he acts in the play, Stephen is aware that the girl Emma (E.C.) is in the audience. He hopes to see her after the play. But only his family waits at the theater door. Bitterly disappointed, he runs off by himself, wandering the streets like a wounded animal—the recurrent motif of walking the streets to find a solution. He is finally calmed by the squalor of his surroundings—"horse piss and rotted straw."

NOTE: Here Joyce reminds you of how important the sense of smell is to Stephen. Of all the senses, it seems the earthiest, the least intellectual and most sensual, and the most closely tied to everyday human life. Throughout the book, smells—even unpleasant smells—will calm Stephen, make him feel connected to the real world.

Visit to Cork

A trip to Cork with his father heightens Stephen's misgivings about his father. They have come to this city in the south of Ireland, where his father grew up, to sell the last of his property to keep the family solvent.

For Simon, it's a nostalgic return to his past. With old cronies, he relives his younger days as a dashing playboy. But for Stephen, it's a painful experience. He watches his father fritter away in bars the meager sum he has just collected for the property. Simon's drunken bragging and sentimentality humiliate his son. Once again, Stephen turns inward into his own emotions.

NOTE: Joyce's own father was brought up in Cork. Like Simon Dedalus, he was high-spirited, an athlete, and a man-about-town. He sang well and acted with flair. For a short time, he attended medical school in Cork—as Simon did—but failed.

Joyce's brother Stanislaus points out in his honest and moving memoir, *My Brother's Keeper*, that when James took this trip to Cork with his father, he was actually amused rather than angry. In real life, Joyce was patient with his father. He became more and more like his father in his love of singing and drinking, and in his skill at dodging creditors. He even tried medical school in Paris for a short while.

Well-chosen details bring to life the little country town, its local speech and gentle humor. But Stephen is not amused. He feels only a cold detachment. Although the withdrawn, prudish youth envies the sociability and lustiness of his father's circle, no life or youthful spirit stirs within him. Simon rubs it in by boasting that he's a better man than his son.

Do you feel sorry for this isolated, unhappy young man? Or do you merely feel impatient with him as he struggles "against the squalor of his life and against the riot of his mind"?

One emotion Stephen does feel now that he's a bit older is "a cold and cruel loveless lust." In the anatomy lecture hall of his father's old college, Stephen spies the word "foetus" carved on a desk. This triggers guilty feelings about his (own) "mad and filthy orgies" (probably masturbation but possibly just erotic fantasies). Do you think Stephen would feel quite as much guilt in today's more sexually informed climate?

Just what "foetus" means to Stephen, and why the word arouses his guilt, has been debated. Stephen is still an adolescent. His sexual drives are strong, but he hasn't acted on them. Because his religious training has taught him that the physical is inferior to the spiritual, he's often wrapped up his sexual thoughts in romanticized longings for a girl as pure as the Virgin Mary.

The word "foetus" is a blunt reminder of the physical side of sex. It's a reminder of the consequences of sex, consequences Stephen may not be ready to think about, much less accept. Because the sound of words is always important to Stephen, as it is to Joyce, the nearness in sound of "foetus" to "fetid" (having an offensive smell) may increase his squeamishness.

In addition, Stephen may see the word as a crude medical term for a human being. He seems to imagine that the medical students who jokingly scrawled it on the desk are oafs lacking sensitivity toward human life. (In *Ulysses*, Stephen will be surrounded by such medical students.) And because his father was once a medical student here, the word and the images it inspires also seem to bring back all Stephen's dislike for Simon Dedalus' crude good nature.

The trip to Cork is an important step in Stephen's development. He faces his father's failures—a first step toward rejection of parental authority. He also acknowledges his own unromantic sexual drives.

Sexual Initiation
The tormented youth is enjoying a rare moment of good cheer. He is in high spirits because he has won a substantial cash prize for scoring high in an examination and for writing an essay.

NOTE: The prize money was £30 for his "exhibition" (outstanding work) in the exam and £3 for his essay in the annual examination given at all secondary schools in Ireland. You may think £33 a paltry sum. In those days, it was the equivalent of nine months of a teacher's salary. And the academic honor was great.

The money gives Stephen a taste of power and a temporary lift. He brightens the dreary family life by spending freely on food and clothes. He attends the theater with friends, like a man-about-town. He redoes his room with a pot of pink paint— a symbol of rosy hopes.

Why does money seem to cure Stephen's problems? Could it be, as some think, that they are mainly economic? Is Joyce saying that Stephen would have fewer problems if his family hadn't become poor? Joyce himself struggled with poverty long after he left Ireland and was in a good position to be realistic about it.

The orgy of spending ends all too soon, and Stephen's misery returns. Stephen's pot of pink paint was not enough to finish redoing his room, just as his money was not sufficient to solve his problems. Notice in what form the color pink returns before the end of the chapter.

Stephen is again consumed by sexual fantasies. He indulges in erotic activities (masturbation) he calls "secret riots." In Catholic terms, these put him in a state of mortal sin. This is a heavy burden for a still-religious boy. "Brutal words" now spring from him. He contrasts his present state with his earlier, innocent longing for Mercedes and the soft speeches of Claude Melnotte, the romantic hero of *The Lady of Lyons* by English writer Edward Bulwer-Lytton.

If you are puzzled by the intensity of Stephen's sexual frustration, remember that in late nineteenth-century Ireland, and in other countries, there were strict notions about the immorality of masturbation, illicit sexual relations, or even about close physical contact of any kind.

Stephen again searches himself for answers by walking through the maze of Dublin's "dark slimy streets." In the tradition of the literary realism he admired, Joyce stresses the sordid details of Stephen's walk. Images recur that reflect Stephen's despondency: the maze of the streets and the yellow (decay) gas flames. In a section of town filled with brothels, a young prostitute stops Stephen, takes him to her room, and enfolds the trembling youth in a sensual embrace. He gratefully surrenders at last.

The "magic moment" of romance with a real Mercedes that Stephen longed for earlier becomes in fact a whore's embrace. The white, rose-covered cottage is a tawdry room with an obscene doll. But the prostitute is almost motherly. Her room is "warm and lightsome"; her dress is—like the pot of paint—pink. Is Joyce saying there is hope and romance in the real world? Or is he saying that, symbolically, what Stephen was searching for was not romance but sexual release?

The language of this segment is richly evocative and sensual. Words can make the sordid beautiful. To Stephen, the whore's kiss is "darker than the swoon of sin, softer than sound or odour." The combination of sensations (of sight, touch, sound, and smell), along with the repetitive sound of the letter "s," have led some to call this an overly poetic and overwritten passage. Others find that this poetic language accurately expresses Stephen's desire to find romance—to beautify his experience. Do you think Joyce may have purposely overwritten the seduction scene in order to poke fun at Stephen's romantic nature?

The chapter that began in country innocence ends in urban squalor and sin. Stephen has finally given in to his body and acknowledged his passions, an apparent triumph over fear. But, as in his boyish triumph at Clongowes, the sense of victory will be short-lived.

CHAPTER THREE

This chapter is one long sequence of sin, remorse, and repentence, a reaction to Stephen's new-found sexual freedom. Guilt-ridden, Stephen succumbs to the temptation to fall back into the comforting but constricting arms of mother Church.

The Sinner

Stephen has changed between the end of Chapter Two and the beginning of Chapter Three. (Joyce doesn't make it clear how much time has elapsed between the two chapters—perhaps only a few months, perhaps as much as a year. Stephen's craving for "bruised potatoes" and fat hunks of mutton (a robust Irish stew) is the symbol of his gross new life of lust. At night he wallows in the low world of prostitutes. But his first sexual rapture has waned. Be sure to notice how carefully Joyce's language parallels Stephen's disillusionment. No more poetic passages describe Stephen's activities. The style is blunt and the tone is realistic—the beer-stained tables, the coarse solicitations of the prostitutes.

In sin, Stephen seems to have found a "dark peace." He thinks he is accepting his state of mortal sin coolly. But his subconscious mind creates images of chaos. A math equation turns into a peacock's tail unfolding itself like his soul, sin by sin.

NOTE: The key words repeated to convey Stephen's guilty mood in this section are "dull," "dark," "dusk," and "cold." As he repents later, the words will change to "grey," "white," and "pale"—all images of cleanliness and purity.

If you have ever denied feelings of guilt and tried

to pretend you didn't care, like Stephen, you know it's hard to stifle these feelings completely. Stephen is aware that he is guilty not only of lust, but of the other six "deadly sins," especially that of pride. He even seems to take pride in his own sins.

NOTE: The seven deadly sins   By long Christian tradition, the seven deadly (cardinal) sins are lust, anger, gluttony, covetousness, envy, pride, and sloth. Their nature and consequence was explained most famously in St. Thomas Aquinas' thirteenth-century work, *Summa Theologica*. To be guilty of one of these failings in thought, word, or deed is to be in a state of mortal sin. Merely feeling remorse will not help the sinner. He or she must confess, receive absolution, and do penance.

Stephen has stopped going to Mass—to go to Mass in a state of mortal sin is to commit the further sin of sacrilege. But he takes a perverse pleasure in contemplating the Church doctrines he has violated, and he continues to serve as leader (prefect) of the Sodality of the Blessed Virgin Mary, one of the college's two devotional societies, which meets in church on Saturdays. The prefect is supposed to be an exemplary Catholic, observing the rules of behavior and the rites of confession and Communion. At times, the gentle image of the Virgin in the church makes him consider repentance.

The Retreat
The rector of Belvedere announces a three-day retreat, a period devoted to religious meditation. This prospect strikes terror into Stephen's heart. He ob-

viously feels more guilt than he will admit to himself. The hold of religion is still strong.

NOTE: A retreat is an exercise in religious meditation. It is based on the model set up by the founder of the Jesuit order, Saint Ignatius of Loyola. This retreat is in honor of Saint Francis Xavier, a sixteenth-century Jesuit priest known for his missionary work in India and the Far East.

The retreat master is Clongowes' Father Arnall. He has aged since Stephen left. Seeing him reminds Stephen of his early years at Clongowes, and he recalls the innocence of his childhood.

Father Arnall opens the retreat by telling the boys that the most important thing in the world is the salvation of one's soul. He prays that if any poor soul in the audience is in mortal sin, the retreat will be the turning point in his life. He promises to speak of the "four last things"—death, judgment, hell, and heaven. (Joyce doesn't choose to record the sermon on heaven, which doesn't suit his purpose, to show how frightened Stephen is of hell.)

Arnall's sermons on death and judgment chill Stephen's soul. When the day of judgment comes, God will know the truth, and Stephen will be exposed in front of all those he has deceived. On that terror-filled day, it will be too late to repent.

Stephen is convinced that every word of the sermon is aimed at him. He is ashamed of his sexual excesses. He feels he has defiled Emma—and other women—in his lustful thoughts. In his anguish, he takes comfort in the Virgin Mary, refuge of sin-

ners. He even imagines that she joins his hands
and Emma's in a gesture of peace.

Sermon on Hell
Father Arnall's sermons increase in power and elo-
quence. He recounts the fall of the angel Lucifer
(Satan), and then of Adam and Eve.

The priest describes graphically the horrors and
physical torments of hell. In the eternal darkness,
the sinners' senses will suffer and worms will gnaw
at their eyes (a harkening back to the threat of
blindness in the prelude). Stephen suffers men-
tally all the torments that Arnall describes so vividly.

NOTE: Fallen angel In this version of creation,
Lucifer and his rebellious angels were hurled down
to hell, because they defied God. Lucifer, the fallen
angel of light, was another name for Satan, or the
devil. John Milton (1608–74) used this myth in his
epic poem *Paradise Lost*. Later on, Stephen will use
the Latin form of Lucifer's words, *"Non serviam"*
("I will not serve"), as his own defiant motto. Some
therefore see Stephen as taking on the identity of
Lucifer. Like him, Stephen will be a fallen angel
renouncing God as well as country and family.

In another sermon on hell, the relentless Arnall
continues to fuel Stephen's anguish with threats
of the everlasting spiritual torments of eternal punishment. Arnall ends with a ringing call for repentance.

NOTE: Sermons on hell Arnall's sermons and
language are largely derived from the tracts (reli-

gious pamphlets) of a seventeenth-century Jesuit, Giovanni Pinamonti, that were translated in the nineteenth century. Joyce rewrote and tailored Pinamonti's text to suit his needs.

Arnall's sermons are meant to put the fear of damnation into his audience by painting frightening scenes and using grossly graphic, unpleasant physical details. This technique is, as he says, called "composition of place" and is taken from the founder of the Jesuits, Ignatius of Loyola. Some Catholic observers have objected to Arnall's sermons as not wholly in keeping with Church dogma. Scholars have pointed out inaccuracies. But other readers consider the sermons samples of Joyce's most effective writing, writing that inspires terror but also makes you wonder about the kind of narrow, rigid mind that would seek to inspire such terror.

___

The two sermons on hell, its physical torments and its spiritual torments, form the climax of the retreat. They also form the moral center of the novel. They provide the vision of the world, of God, and of the universe, which Stephen must accept or reject. Stephen believes that if he accepts and repents his sins, he will be a good Catholic, a good Irishman, a good son—but never, perhaps, an artist. If he rejects the sermon, he may gain his artistic freedom—but at the risk of losing his soul. For now, guilt is winning out over defiance.

Confession and Redemption

Back in his room, the remorseful Stephen suffers a frightening vision of his own hell crowded with lecherous, goatlike fiends prowling among stinking weeds reeking with odors of dung. (Like Father Arnall's, this hell, too, involves the punishment of all the senses.) The horror of the vision is so real that a spasm of vomiting overcomes Stephen.

"Repent!" and "Confess!" are now added to the "Apologise!" and "Admit!" of earlier chapters. Stephen may have his spells of independence, but he is still not free of religion—and guilt.

Stephen stumbles out into the evening, determined to go to confession before he returns home for supper. As he did at the end of the last chapter, Stephen walks about at random until he finds a church in a poor neighborhood, where he is unknown. In an agony of shame, he finally confesses to a gentle Capuchin monk—a contrast to the threatening Arnall. His "prideful and lustful" rebellion is over—for the moment.

NOTE: Capuchins, a branch of Franciscan monks, were named for the Italian word for the cowl (*cappuchio*) of their robes. They were known in Dublin as strict but kindly confessors, and here they provide a glimpse of a Catholic Church that is simpler but more humane than the Jesuit-dominated church you've seen up to now.

Stephen now feels his soul is purified. He strides home, elated. Even the muddy streets seem cheerful to him. He comes back to a peaceful kitchen scene, the symbol of his return to a conventional life. In school the next day, he kneels with a clear conscience at the altar. Reborn to a life of virtue, he is now able to take Communion with them without committing sacrilege. Again, the chapter ends with Stephen's feeling victorious. Virtue has apparently triumphed over sin.

NOTE: White is the symbol of Stephen's new purity of mind. The meal he comes back to is white: white pudding and white eggs. The flowers on the altar are white, "clear and silent as his own soul." Do you think Joyce's use of "white" here and earlier is meant to symbolize virtue? Or is it a comment on how pale and neutral Stephen's life might be now?

Do you think Stephen will remain virtuous? If he did, this return to grace would be the climax of his adolescent life. But you'll see that it merely follows the pattern of earlier chapters. Conflicts end in apparent victories, but so far these have only been temporary.

CHAPTER FOUR

This chapter concerns Stephen's return to piety and his renewed doubts about religion. It ends with the climactic revelation of his true calling.

Devotion

The Stephen you now see is not the lustful lad who craved mutton stew at the beginning of Chapter Three. The devout new Stephen dedicates his waking hours to prayers and religious ritual. He punishes his senses by fasting, by walking with his eyes downcast, and by sitting in uncomfortable positions, in the cold. (Notice, though, that he has trouble mortifying his sense of smell. For both Stephen and Joyce, all smells are associated with life,

and if you value life you can't find them unpleasant.) The trials he imposes on himself make him
feel he is sharing the suffering of the saints, like
his namesake, the martyred Stephen.

However, despite all his efforts at self-abase-
ment and obedience, Stephen's flawed individuality asserts itself in the form of doubt, irritability,
and stand-offishness. He becomes angry at his
mother's sneezing; he feels unable to humbly
"merge his life in the common tide of other lives;"
he is again beset by "voices of the flesh." His attempts to understand spiritual love, which he seeks
in a certain work by Saint Alphonsus Liguori, ends
in sensual desire.

NOTE: Saint Alphonsus was a noted eighteenth-
century missionary. His book, *Visits to the Most
Blessed Sacrament*, contains quotations from the
Canticle of Canticles, which in the King James ver-
sion of the Old Testament is called the Song of
Solomon. The sensual language and imagery of
the Canticle is given a spiritual interpretation by
Catholicism and other Christian denominations.

Stephen ends up doubting the sincerity of his
own repentance, since it may have been only a
response to the fear of doom Father Arnall's sermons had inspired.

Doubts about the Priesthood
Subtle temptation comes to Stephen in a dramatic
scene with the director of studies at Belvedere. The
director is so impressed by Stephen's piety that he
feels the youth should think of becoming a mem-

ber of the Jesuit order—considered a great privilege. It's a friendly talk. Yet there seems to be something ominous about it. Why does the director dangle and loop the cord of the window blind? Is it meant to suggest a noose? Is it a symbolic warning that the priesthood is suffocating, a form of death? What other details do you notice in this scene that add to the feeling of gloom?

Stephen is also put off by the director's small talk about the Capuchins' robes, called in Belgium "jupes" (French for skirts). He seems to be calling the Capuchins effeminate. To Stephen, the director's rivalry with another order is mean and unbecoming, especially because it was a Capuchin confessor who showed Stephen kindness in the last chapter.

Stephen is flattered by the director's offer. He is also tempted by the thought of the priesthood's power and protection from sin. Stephen is well aware of his pride, as he is of his lack of love for others. The word "proud" is used repeatedly in this chapter. He imagines himself learning great secrets and small ones. Hearing confession, the sins of others will be revealed while he as a priest stands apart, uncontaminated. As a natural outsider with a sense of his own superior intellectual gifts, Stephen seems well suited to the Jesuit order.

But Stephen also sees another side of the priesthood. As he takes his leave of the director, he sees the priest's face as "a mirthless mask reflecting a sunken day." This evokes for him the grave, chilly life he would lead as a priest. In contrast, some young men passing by are stepping lightly to a musical tune. What is Joyce suggesting by this contrast?

As he walks along, he tries to sort out his emotions. Passing by the house where the Jesuits live, he remembers his days at Clongowes and he realizes, in a sudden moment of revelation (epiphany), that order and obedience are not his destiny. He will bypass the temptations of the Church. He foresees that he will yield to sin again. Like Lucifer, he will fall, but the fall will make him a part of the real world.

Back home, Stephen finds that his family is being evicted again. The kitchen gardens stink of rotten cabbages. But the odor pleases him. (Once again you see that to Stephen and to Joyce, smells are almost always positive symbols of earthy human life.)

The kitchen itself is littered with scraps of bread, and jars used as teacups, indications of the family's deepening poverty. It's a bleak setting. But Stephen smiles. He finds new beauty in this setting; it is the real world. He realizes he prefers the "disorder, the misrule and confusion of his father's house" to the austere order of the priesthood. His smile as he sings along with his brothers and sisters is a contrast to the Jesuit's "mirthless mask." The children's music is the music of earth and of real life—like the rotting cabbages.

Self-Discovery

Now that Stephen has rejected the life of a priest, he plans to go to University College in Dublin against his mother's wishes. Stephen is also in the process of freeing himself from his mother, whose religious orientation leads her to fear the free, intellectual life that the university represents. She knows it will pull him away from her and the Church.

Again, Stephen walks restlessly. This time he goes toward the Bull, a seawall, or breakwater, that extends into Dublin Bay. As he walks, he hears the music of an "elfin prelude," wild and fast, and the sound of hoofs racing on the grass.

NOTE: The elfin prelude suggests the music of Claude Debussy, the late nineteenth-century French composer. He was linked artistically with Stéphane Mallarmé and other poets of the Symbolist literary movement that Joyce admired. This prelude may refer to Debussy's "Prelude to the Afternoon of a Faun," based on a Mallarmé poem.

A group of Christian Brothers pass him on a wooden bridge. He feels scorn for their uncouth, weatherbeaten faces and their plain names. They are a symbol of prosaic, dull Dublin—and therefore of Ireland. He is ashamed of his intolerance. But they seem like low, earthbound creatures, and he is ready to leave their world.

As he walks on the seawall called the Bull, Stephen watches the swift-moving clouds. He remembers a favorite poetic phrase—"a day of dappled seaborne clouds"—which makes him aware of his joy in words. The drifting clouds are moving beyond Ireland to the mainland of Europe, just as Stephen will set out to do later.

Stephen's musings about words are significant. They tell you what he feels is the writer's art. Language has power—and Stephen covets this power. Words can do more than depict the surface color of life. They are the tools for revealing the deeper, elusive "inner world of individual emotions."

A group of boys Stephen knows, who have been swimming off the Bull, playfully call to him. "Come along, Dedalus! Bous Stephanoumenos! Bous Stephaneforos!" As Stephen looks at their naked wet bodies, they seem cold and characterless. But the names they call out seem prophetic.

NOTE: Stephen's names   The boys' wordplay comes from the Greek. "Bous" means "ox"; the name Stephen means "a garland." The boys are shouting, "ox-wreathed," "ox-garlanded." In part, they're showing off their schoolboy learning. The references are also linked to locale. The seawall they stand on is called the Bull; Stephen has just come from Clontarf Chapel—in Gaelic, Clontarf means "the field of the bull." And by calling Stephen a bull, by referring to him as wreathed and garlanded—as if in celebration—they contribute to the sense of triumph and victory building in this scene.

Stephen's last name is even more laden with meaning. As he's beginning to understand, he shares it with "the fabulous artificer" of Greek myth, Daedalus. You're about to see the impact this sudden understanding has upon Stephen. Daedalus, too, is linked to the image of bulls. The maze he created was designed to contain the Minotaur, half-bull and half-man; it was from the Minotaur that he and his son, Icarus, escaped by means of their wax wings. Perhaps Stephen is both bull and artificer, both menace and the means of escape from that menace, his own worst enemy and his own best hope.

As Stephen hears his names called, he has a vision of a hawk-like man flying above the sea. He understands at last that, like hawk-like Daedalus, he is destined to be a creative artist. This is the call to which all his development, struggles, and doubts have been leading. He triumphantly rejects "the world of duties and despair," and "the pale service of the altar." He will exchange the power of the priesthood for the power of artistic creation—the priesthood of art.

The moment is one of rebirth, with Stephen's soul resurrected "from the grave of boyhood" to creative maturity. It's a moment of revelation, the book's central epiphany, which Joyce describes in intensely poetic terms.

Just as Stephen is breathlessly accepting the legacy of his namesake, Daedalus, one of the swimmers cries out: "O, cripes, I'm drownded!" This ominous cry echoes the old hag (of Chapter One) when Casey spit in her eye: "I'm blinded and drownded!" It also recalls the fate of Icarus, son of Daedalus, who fell into the sea because he flew too close to the sun with his wax wings. Stephen will try to soar and escape the labyrinth like Daedalus, the father. But he may fly too high and fall, like Icarus, the son.

NOTE: Sea and water imagery You'll notice how much of this scene is filled with images of water and the sea, from the bodies of Stephen's friends that "gleamed with the wet of the sea," to the waves the dim, hawk-like figure flies above, to the call, "I'm drownded!" Sea and water have played an important symbolic role throughout the book. Earlier they usually (but not always) indicated dirt and impurity. Now their meaning is changing, perhaps from the force of Stephen's revelation. Water can still be a threatening element—Icarus drowned in the sea. But it can also be a symbol of richness and life. Here Joyce seems to be powerfully linking the sea to Stephen's rebirth as an artist. It's as if Stephen has been reborn and is now being baptized.

At the height of his ecstasy, Stephen sees a girl wading on the beach. She has the appearance of a strange and beautiful seabird. The girl is physically beautiful but unashamed; she is also compared to an "angel of mortal youth and beauty." Both a bird of the spirit and a sensual sea creature, she seems to fuse together, like the females before her, Stephen's ideals of womanhood—passionate and spiritual. Only this time, the spiritual side is not totally virginal and sexless, and the sensuality is not unrestrained but natural and healthy. This angel is sturdy and earthbound. She returns Stephen's gaze calmly.

NOTE: The girl wading   The girl Stephen sees wading is one of the most powerful images in *Portrait of the Artist*. "A strange and beautiful seabird," she fuses two important symbols. As a bird, she symbolizes the creative freedom represented a few pages earlier by Stephen's vision of "a hawklike man." As a creature of the sea, she's linked to the power of the sea to give Stephen a new life as an artist.

Stephen's vision also has religious overtones. In some ways, she's a version of his worshipped Virgin Mary; her slate-blue skirts, for example, are the color associated with the Virgin. But rather than representing Catholicism, she represents Stephen's new, secular religion: art. "Heavenly God," Stephen cries out. But he cries "in an outburst of profane [ungodly] joy"—a sign his vision is not Christian but earthly.

You can also see the girl as Stephen's Muse, his artistic inspiration. And perhaps she's a symbol of the sexual joy Stephen hopes to find in his new life, a mermaid who trails seaweed and with her siren call lures Stephen toward a world of sensuality. Because Stephen calls her "a dark plumed dove," some readers feel she represents his desire for a merger of religious peace and earthly, sensual love.

Stephen walks off across the beach, singing and calling out to life. Later, he falls asleep, exhausted, his soul "swooning" into some new world.

This scene of Stephen's double ecstatic visions— the first of the creative artificer who shares his name, the second of the young girl who calls him to art— is generally considered the climax of the novel. Stephen has found his path. Notice, too, how this triumphant final scene follows the pattern established in earlier chapters. From a low point at the beginning of the chapter, Stephen has risen again to victory. He has gone from self-doubt to self-discovery. Will he plunge again into despair before he is ready at last to fly from the nest?

CHAPTER FIVE

Just as Chapter One introduced the major themes and motifs, this last chapter recalls them, expands them, and ties them together.

Now that Stephen has been converted to the religion of art, he is pursuing his goal of becoming a literary figure. As a student at the university, he debates with fellow students and teachers many issues, such as Irish nationalism, his family, and the Church. You'll also see some evidence of his artistic and intellectual development: his theory of art and an ambitious poem. The diary excerpts at the end sum up Stephen's attitudes and express his final revolt.

University Student

The exalted youth flying high at the end of the last chapter is now down to earth in the usual transitional pattern of rise and fall from one chapter to the next. In his shabby, untidy house, he is breakfasting on a meager meal of watery tea and crusts of fried bread, a sharp contrast to the festive Christmas meal of the first chapter. He is still under his parents' wings. His mother grumbles as she washes his neck. His father whistles for him and curses him. As Stephen, resentful, walks to the university through littered streets, he is clearly ready to fly away on his own. Have you had days in which family life seems unbearable, as it does to Stephen? Dublin and his family are offending "the pride of his youth."

The thoughts that swirl in Stephen's mind as he walks to class give us clues to his present feelings and describe some earlier university scenes. You'll notice how important literature has become to him. The Dublin streets bring to mind scenes written by his favorite writers: Gerhart Hauptmann, a German playwright (1862–1946); the previously mentioned John Henry Cardinal Newman; the thirteenth-century Italian poet Guido Cavalcanti; Joyce's own hero, Norwegian playwright Henrik Ibsen (1828–1906); the seventeenth-century English writer Ben Jonson. Language, too, fills his mind, as you see in the word plays on ivy and ivory. You also see glimpses of his classmates—the idealistic MacCann, Cranly, the "confessor" Stephen tells of "all the tumults and unrest and longing in his soul," and Davin, the Irish "peasant" and fervent nationalist.

NOTE: Stephen's friends   Many of Stephen's friends are modeled after people in Joyce's own student circle. George Clancy (Davin) was killed by British government troops while he was mayor of Limerick during Ireland's fight for independence. Francis Skeffington (MacCann) was also killed by British troops, during the Easter rebellion of 1916. J.F. Byrne (Cranly) was Joyce's closest friend until his disapproval of Joyce's bawdy behavior in Paris earned Joyce's anger. (As a result, Cranly is portrayed as being prim and perhaps homosexual, which Byrne was not.) Soon you'll meet Lynch, modeled after Joyce's close friend Vincent Cosgrave. This portrait, too , is biased: Joyce bore Cosgrave a grudge for standing aside while Joyce was involved in a street brawl; Cosgrave was also a brief and unsuccessful rival for the affections of Nora Barnacle. When the annoyed Joyce wrote about Cosgrave in *Portrait of the Artist*, he gave him the name of an evil Irish mayor who hanged his own son. In 1927 Cosgrave/Lynch was found drowned (a presumed suicide) in London's Thames River, fulfilling Joyce's prediction that his life would be a failure.

Stephen finds himself haunted by a story Davin has told him. While walking the countryside on a dark night, Davin knocked at a house for a glass of water and was greeted by a young woman. Half-naked, perhaps pregnant, she asks him to spend the night. Davin, tempted, is "all in a fever," but he flees.

Why does Davin's story strike Stephen so strongly? Perhaps partly because it was told by Davin, who has an innocence and a simplicity Stephen knows he lacks. Partly, too, the woman seems to represent an Ireland that Stephen finds both seductive and disturbing. The milk she offers Davin links her to the moocow and other cows that represented Ireland earlier in the book—the often beautiful but finally stifling Ireland Stephen must reject. She's also been compared to fallen Eve tempting still-innocent Adam. Like so many other images in *Portrait of the Artist*, her symbolic meaning is ambiguous but powerful nonetheless.

At the university, as in his former schools, Stephen feels alienated. A conversation with the dean of studies increases this feeling. As the dean lights a fire, he and Stephen discuss the useful arts—such as fire-starting—versus the liberal arts. Is a fire beautiful only if it is useful? Stephen stands on the side of pure beauty. In support of his stand, he quotes the thirteenth-century religious thinker, Saint Thomas Aquinas, his favorite philosopher. In the end, the dean patronizingly advises Stephen to focus on practical matters before flying off in pursuit of art and beauty. Stephen doesn't. For him, the dean is "an unlit lamp," a cleric with a closed mind. Once again, he is disappointed in the priests—the fathers, like his own, who prove themselves false. The encounter with the dean sets the stage for Stephen's later statement of a theory of art based on Aquinas.

In physics class, too, Stephen feels isolated as his fellow students crack good-humored, bawdy jokes. He will not sign his friend MacCann's petitions for world peace and disarmament. He also rejects Davin's efforts to involve him in Irish cultural affairs, like the revival of the Gaelic language and indigenous Irish sports. His ideological friends berate him. MacCann calls him "a minor poet," who has a lot to learn about his social obligations. "Try to be one of us," says Davin. "Be a poet or mystic later." He also faults Stephen for being a loner—"a born sneerer."

In fact, Stephen shares some of his friends' concerns. Like Davin, he worries if the English language imposed on Ireland by conquerors can ever be truly his—as you see during his discussion of the words "tundish" and "funnel" with the dean. But to Stephen, his calling as an artist means that he must not become embroiled in social issues. Besides, he has little patience for Ireland. His country does not deserve his concern. She has betrayed her heroes, from Wolfe Tone to Parnell. She is "the old sow that eats her farrow." He will not be eaten. "You talk to me of nationality, language, religion. I shall try to fly by those nets."

If you agree with Davin that Stephen is a prideful egotist, you may condemn his rejection of worthy causes. Do you agree with Stephen that an artist should separate his work from social concerns?

NOTE: Joyce himself was not completely unconcerned with politics; he called himself a Socialist in principle. In general, though, he thought an artist should stick to the concerns of the spirit, and he devoted his life to the intense, lonely, and ill-paid labor of writing (and defending) his unconventional books.

Theory of Art

As a self-proclaimed priest of art, Stephen needs his own dogma—a system of belief. He claims to base his aesthetic views on those formulated by Aquinas.

Stephen's aesthetic discussions are among the most complex and intellectually demanding sections in *Portrait of the Artist*. Many readers have debated their meaning, wondering whether Joyce shared Stephen's theories or whether he wanted to show them to be inconsistent and immature.

To make Stephen's long discussion easier to understand, Joyce has Stephen expound his theory to Lynch, whose down-to-earth responses to Stephen's high-minded discourse provide comic relief by poking fun at his friend's solemn literary pretensions. Some think that Lynch is really the voice of Joyce taking the opportunity to mock his own youthful dependence on Jesuit modes of philosophy, modes that give Stephen's theory "the true scholastic stink." (The word "scholastic" refers not only to school in general, but in particular to medieval philosophy that was based on the Church fathers and Aristotle, especially as the two were combined in the writings of Aquinas.)

Stephen begins by saying that the feelings inspired by true art are *static*, unmoving, while the feelings inspired by untrue, improper art are *ki-*

netic, or moving. Improper art excites the emotions; it urges us to go out and do something. For example, art that is improper and didactic (designed to morally instruct) might be intended to make us sign a petition, join a worthy cause. At the other extreme, pornography is improper art because it seeks to inspire us to commit acts of lust.

Proper art, however, doesn't inspire us to do anything: it raises the mind above desire and loathing to a purer state. (Aristotle called this result catharsis.)

What do you think of Stephen's distinction between proper and improper art? Can you name any works of art (literature, painting, or music) that Stephen might categorize as improper? How would you defend them?

Stephen goes on to say that true art is beautiful and that beauty and truth are closely related. Truth appeals to the intellect and beauty to the imagination.

Again quoting Aquinas, Stephen says that while people's taste in beauty may vary, all beautiful objects must meet three requirements. They must possess wholeness, harmony, and radiance. Wholeness (*integritas*) means that the object at first presents itself to the observer as a single image, a complete whole. After that, the object is seen to possess harmony, *consonantia*. That is, the complete whole is seen to be made up of many separate parts, but the parts are so well-balanced and arranged that they form a unity. The third quality, radiance—*claritas*—is the most difficult to define; it can be seen as the product of the first two qualities. A beautiful object makes you see it as a single whole; then it makes you see it as a harmonious composition of many parts. Finally it makes you understand that this wholeness and harmony could only have been achieved in one way. The object is unique. It could not exist in any other form. That's radiance, the "whatness" of a thing.

Goaded by the laughing Lynch, Stephen further refines his theory. Even among true works of art one must make distinctions. Art can be categorized as lyric, epic, and dramatic. The lyric form expresses the emotions of the artist only; it's a completely personal narrative. The epic form expresses the emotions of characters other than the artist, but the presence of the artist remains continually visible in the narrative. In the dramatic form the artist vanishes completely. Only his characters appear. You can think of these three forms as proceeding from the personal to the semi-personal to the impersonal. One work can contain more than one form. Some readers have called *Portrait of the Artist* essentially lyric. Would you agree or disagree? Does it contain other forms as well?

Stephen's speech on art is not a mere sideshow, as some readers contend. Even if Joyce doesn't want you to agree with Stephen's theories, he wants to show that Stephen has a right to some intellectual pretensions. His theory has already made his reputation on campus, and it's one of the reasons Stephen's friends tolerate his aloofness.

Villanelle

Now Stephen puts his theory into practice by creating his own work of art. The tone of this section is lyrical, in contrast to the dry prose he used earlier to explain his aesthetic theory.

Emma has been on his mind. He has been bitter about what he thinks is a flirtation between her and a young priest. Now he wonders whether he has judged her too harshly. He wakes up near dawn, "dewy wet" after an enchanted night's dream. (Some read this to mean he has had a wet dream.) His room is squalid, but the glow of "a rose and ardent light" (another image of sexual arousal) inspires him to write a poem. As he scribbles the first lines, he relives his relationship with the girl he is writing about, from their first ride together on the streetcar to the recent incident that aroused his jealousy. He resents the fact that she will speak freely into the priest's "latticed ear" (an image of the grille that separates priest and parishioner in the confessional booth) rather than to him, "a priest of the eternal imagination."

Stephen's emotions, as in his theory of lyric expression, are the raw material of his poem. You see the process of creation as thoughts become images and words fall into rhythmic patterns. The poem is in the form of a villanelle.

NOTE: A villanelle is a poem made up of five 3-line stanzas (tercets) and one 4-line stanza (quatrain), all using only two rhymes. The lines are repeated in a regular pattern: a-b-a (five times) and a-b-a-a (one time). The form was popular in the 1890s. This poem—or a version of it—was actually written by Joyce prior to *Portrait of the Artist* and was originally entitled "The Villanelle of the Temptress." Another well-known twentieth-century villanelle is "If I Could Tell You," by the British poet, W.H. Auden.

To finish his poem, Stephen turns Emma into a temptress. She is luring the fallen angel Lucifer, who is also Stephen. (He will compare himself again to Lucifer later on.) The images in this section are lush and sexual: scarlet flowers, rose light, broken cries, lavish limbs, and the "liquid life" of water. He offers the woman a "chalice" (his body) of worship, as a reminder of his rival for Emma's affection, Father Moran, and perhaps to connect her with the Virgin Mary.

The villanelle has an important place in *Portrait of the Artist*. What you think of it as a poem will greatly influence what you think of Stephen. You've seen Stephen reject family, country, and church for art. You've seen him propose elaborate theories of aesthetics. Now, for the first time, you see an example of the art he's thought so much about, the art he's given up so much to create. You'll have to judge: is the villanelle worth his struggles?

It's a question that has inspired much debate. Some readers have scoffed at the poem. They feel that while the verses are technically skillful, they're too imitative of French verse forms and prove that Stephen is only a clever, pretentious scribbler. Other readers, however, make allowances for the villanelle as an immature but very promising effort. And still others regard it as brilliant, finding within it many layers of meaning. Where do you stand?

Preparation for Flight

The rest of Chapter Five describes Stephen's continued progress toward his goal of separation. A flurry of swallows heralds his own flight. Are they signs of good or evil? Stephen is reminded of Thoth, the Egyptian god of writers, who has the head of a bird, and, again, of the hawk-like Daedalus. (Note that he has abandoned Catholic gods in favor of non-Christian ones.) The swallows also remind him of some lines from a play. They, too, seem prophetic of his coming break with Ireland.

NOTE: The lines that begin, "Bend down your faces . . ." are from W. B. Yeats' play *The Countess Cathleen*, which drew the wrath of the Irish when it first opened. In it, Cathleen sells her soul to the devil in exchange for bread for her starving people. Both nationalists and Catholics protested the play, but Stephen defended it—as did the young Joyce in real life.

When Stephen sees Emma next, she stirs up his senses once more. Now he is jealous of his friend Cranly because of a glance Emma gives him. When Stephen catches a louse on his own neck, he is reminded of his poverty. In his mind, he relinquishes the girl to a clean, hairy-chested athlete who washes daily, unlike the louse-ridden poet that Stephen is. He resents the well-heeled Irish upper class who live in their stately homes, begetting an "ignoble" race. If you feel that Stephen's sense of social inferiority fuels his aloofness, this passage is good evidence.

The students he joins gossip, and banter about science, religion, and history. Their jesting talk reflects the accents and manners of student types. Joyce may be showing us how trivial the Irish students seem to Stephen, and why he can leave them without regret. But much as Joyce may seem to scorn them, he sketches them crisply. Their dialogue enlivens the chapter.

Stephen unburdens himself to Cranly, who has played the role of confessor for him before. Now

Stephen is troubled by a quarrel with his mother.
He has made her weep because he refuses to do
his Easter duty—to go to Mass at Easter and receive Communion. You may have had similar pangs
when taking a stand against your parents on an
issue that matters to them.

NOTE: To receive Communion at Easter is an
important rule of the Catholic Church. But it would
be a mortal sin to do it without first going to
confession.

"I will not serve," Stephen tells Cranly, who in
this scene stands for a reasonable conformity. The
phrase is attributed to Lucifer—Satan—at the time
of his fall. The retreat master used these same words
in Chapter Three. Stephen has now aligned himself with Lucifer, the Fallen Angel (as he did in the
villanelle). His talk with Cranly reveals that Stephen no longer believes in the Catholic faith, but
still respects Church tradition. He does not disbe-
lieve enough to commit a sacrilege—to take Communion without confession.
   Questioned by Cranly, Stephen admits he doesn't
have the capacity for love. He may never have loved
anyone, not even his mother. He feels only toler-
ant contempt for his father, "a praiser of his own
past." He himself has tried to love God but failed.
If you tend to view Stephen as a thorough egotist,
these admissions will prove your point.
   Stephen is now convinced he must go away to
achieve the "unfettered freedom" his spirit craves.
His credo: "I will not serve that in which I no longer
believe whether it call itself my home, my father-

land or my church; and I will try to express myself in some mode of life or art as freely as I can. . . ." He will use the weapons of "silence, exile, and cunning"—*silence* on nationalistic Irish issues, *exile* to the freer atmosphere of the Continent, *cunning* (skill) of the writer. He is pridefully defiant, like Lucifer.

"You poor poet!" Cranly exclaims. In a moment of truth, Cranly reveals his own fear of loneliness. There is a suggestion that Cranly seems to be offering to Stephen more than a normal friendship—a masked reference to homosexuality.

Stephen's diary entries for the five weeks before he leaves form an epilogue that looks back to the prelude of the novel. The style of the entries has a new freedom like Stephen's childish thoughts. They are written in brief snatches of disconnected phrases and thoughts, a sample of the extended interior monologues that Joyce later used in *Ulysses.*

The diary form permits Joyce to tie together loose ends and bring together themes and symbols. Stephen's soul is now free, as is his fancy. He has escaped from the nets that restrained him. He casts off Cranly, who has acted as his priest. When his father suggests that he join a rowing club or study law, he only pretends to listen. As for Emma, he treats her coolly, though on the last day he sees her, he realizes that he likes her—a sign, perhaps, that as he matures he's becoming able to accept women not just as virgins or temptresses, but as people. As he gets ready to leave, his mother tells him she hopes he will learn "what the heart is and what it feels." Do you think Stephen recognizes his incapacity to love as a defect? Or does he consider it another form of restraint?

The next to the last entry is one of the most famous paragraphs of modern prose. "Welcome, O life! I go to encounter for the millionth time the reality of experience and to forge in the smithy of my soul the uncreated conscience of my race."

As an artist, a word-craftsman, Stephen will forge (create with words) out of his personal experience the consciousness (conscience) of his race (Ireland and all mankind). His own experiences will be transformed into a universal message.

Do you feel that this promise is a brave and noble one? Or is it the ultimate statement of Stephen's arrogance and pretentiousness? Joyce was able to hammer the raw material of his youth—Ireland, his family, the Church, and his education—into works that relate to all humanity. Do you think Stephen will be able to do the same?

Portrait of the Artist ends with a beginning. Stephen is ready to emerge as a poet. In the last diary entry, Stephen appeals to his mythical father, Daedalus, who has taken the place of his real father in the prelude. The Irish "moocow" has yielded to the universal myth. Once again, you have to ask yourself, will Stephen become the Daedalus or the Icarus of the myth? Will he fly or drown? If Stephen Dedalus is identified with the young James Joyce, then there are many who would say that he succeeded. But there are also those who would claim the opposite. And, there are others who would say both—that Joyce flew with *Ulysses* and drowned in *Finnegans Wake*.

A final judgment on Stephen/James is unlikely. For more on the subject, proceed to *Ulysses* where Stephen returns to Dublin in search of a new father.

A STEP BEYOND

Tests and Answers

TESTS

Test 1

1. The Christmas dinner scene shows Stephen _____
   that
   A. life is cruel and unfair
   B. Dante sides with the Church against
      Parnell
   C. Parnell was a wicked man

2. John Casey spits in an old woman's eye _____
   because she
   A. called Kitty O'Shea a bad name
   B. was drunk and disorderly
   C. reviled Parnell

3. Heron and his classmates who harass _____
   Stephen represent
   I. the forces of evil
   II. the bigotry of the Church
   III. the pressures of conformity
   A. I and II only   B. II and III only
   C. I and III only

4. Father Dolan pandybats Stephen because _____
   A. Stephen has written a bad Latin
      theme
   B. the pages of his theme are marred by
      inkblots
   C. Stephen appears not to be working

5. A religious retreat is _____

A. a confession of guilt to a priest
B. prayers to a patron saint
C. an interval of religious reflection

6. Stephen runs off after the Whitsuntide play ____
   because
   A. his parents aren't waiting for him
   B. the girl he likes hasn't shown up
   C. he has offended his teachers

7. Davin calls Stephen a "terrible man" ____
   because he
   A. will not join the Gaelic League
   B. refuses to sign a petition for world
      peace
   C. talks against Ireland

8. Stephen's friend Lynch serves as ____
   A. a father confessor to Stephen
   B. comic relief as Stephen lectures on his
      art theory
   C. a political agitator who tries to arouse
      Stephen's national pride

9. Major themes in this novel are ____
   I. revolt against parental authority
   II. doubts about religion
   III. the role of poverty in the making of
        an artist
   A. I and II only   B. I and III only
   C. I, II, and III

10. Stephen's experience with Father Conmee ____
    develops the themes of
    I. the false father
    II. egotism
    III. revolt against religion

A. I and II only   B. II and III only
C. I and III only

11. Discuss the novel's comic and satirical aspects.

12. Explain Joyce's choice of the name "Dedalus" for his hero.

13. Why is Stephen tempted to become a priest? Why does he decide against it?

14. Discuss bird imagery in the novel, from the opening scene to the final diary.

Test 2

1. As a schoolboy, Stephen is puzzled by   _____
   I. where the universe ends
   II. who his father is
   III. what politics mean
   A. I only   B. I and II only
   C. I, II, and III

2. Stephen pours his emotions into a poem   _____
   after the
   I. Christmas dinner
   II. tram ride with E.C.
   III. trip to Cork with his father
   A. I and II only   B. II and III only
   C. I, II, and III

3. Stephen and his father go to Cork for the   _____
   purpose of
   A. having a holiday together
   B. selling the remaining family property
   C. visiting his father's old friends

4. The word "foetus" carved on the anatomy   _____
   theater desk startles Stephen because

A. he suspects his father may have
   carved it
B. it expresses his latent sexual longings
C. it suggests a world of science alien to
   him

5. The mutton stew Stephen's belly craves ———
   refers to his
   A. earthy life in the brothels
   B. family's poverty
   C. favorite Irish dish

6. The main theme of Father Arnall's sermons ———
   is the
   A. life of St. Francis Xavier
   B. fall of Adam and Eve
   C. "four last things"

7. The "old sow that eats her farrow" is ———
   A. Ireland   B. the Church
   C. Woman

8. Stephen echoes Lucifer when he asserts: ———
   A. "Non serviam."
   B. "I am not afraid to make a mistake."
   C. "Welcome, O life!"

9. The symbol of Stephen's vocation as an artist ———
   is the
   A. flight of the swallows
   B. girl on the beach
   C. temptress of the villanelle

10. An important theme in the book is the ———
    I. temptations of the flesh
    II. dullness of Dublin
    III. effect of education on friendship

A. I only   B. I and II only
C. I and III only

11. Compare the roles of Davin, MacCann, and Cranly in Stephen's life.

12. Discuss Stephen's relationship with his mother.

13. Discuss the importance of words and wordplay for Stephen.

14. What is the symbolic role of the girl on the beach in Chapter Five?

ANSWERS

Test 1

1. B	2. A	3. B	4. C	5. C	6. B
7. B	8. B	9. A	10. C		

11. Joyce has been described as an introspective man who had flashes of gaiety and humor. He could always see the droll side of a serious situation.

The story of Stephen's painful development as an artist also has comic moments. It is enlivened from the first chapter to the last with humorous character sketches and dialogues. Even situations that are distressing to Stephen have their comic aspects. The Christmas dinner scene has moments of lusty laughter between Mr. Casey and Mr. Dedalus as they mock churchmen and goad Mrs. Riordan. In contrast to Stephen's gloomy mood during the trip to Cork, his father trades stories and boasts with his cronies in grand Irish style.

You probably chuckled at Uncle Charles in the outhouse scene in Chapter Two and at the grand way he offered the greengrocer's apples to his nephew for his bowels. Joyce's keen ear for dialogue and his mocking wit bring to life the student circle at the university in Chapter Five. Also note the comic aspects of his sketches of Glynn, Goggins, and other students cavorting outside the library.

12. Joyce had signed some of his early pieces "Stephen Daedalus," feeling some closeness with Daedalus, the "fabulous artificer"—skilled craftsman—of Greek legend. He simplified the spelling to "Dedalus" in *A Portrait of the Artist* because it would be more commonplace and believable. (See section on the Daedalus myth.)

Stephen has in common with his namesake a need to find a way out of the labyrinth (maze) of life and to fashion his own means of escape. It is a good metaphor (comparison) for a young man trying to free himself from the restraints of his environment. There are two approaches to the question. Some people restrict the story of Stephen's growing up to the framework of the Daedalus legend. (See the section on Structure.) Others see Stephen more broadly as representing the human race trying to find a way out of life's mazes and mysteries. Joyce does not use the word "labyrinth" in *Portrait of the Artist*, but some readers find the image from the Daedalus legend present in the frequent mention of roads, streets, paths, and corridors. The school corridors are long and dark at Clongowes (Chapter One). In Chapter Two, Stephen wanders through the roads of Blackrock, sorting out his emotions and in Dublin through a "maze of narrow and dirty streets" in search of sexual adventure. In the third chapter, he wanders through the "ill lit streets" at random, searching for a confessor. You will be able to find many other references to reality as a maze.

13. What tempts Stephen most about the priesthood is its secret knowledge and power. He is aware of "the awful power of which angels and saints stood in reverence" (Chapter Four). The director of Belvedere makes this power very clear, pointing out that not even the "Blessed Virgin herself" has the power of the priest to absolve from sin or to make God take the form of bread and wine in the sacrament of Communion.

Stephen has imagined himself as a priest hearing confession and saying Mass. He is intrigued with the dignity of the ritual and of the ceremonial robes. But he is also aware of the contrast between the chilly, ordered, sheltered life of a priest and the warmth of ordinary existence. He chooses the "disorder, the misrule and confusion of his father's house" over the power of the priesthood. You'll find evidence of Stephen's struggle in his interview with the director and his thoughts as he walks home in Chapter Four.

14. The references to birds and bird flight fall into two general categories. Until the retreat in Chapter Three, birds are linked with an element of threat. Note (1) the threatening eagles of the prelude, (2) the football, which is like a "heavy bird" in the Clongowes playground, and (3) the threatening character Heron, with the bird name and the birdlike face, who, like the eagles, demands submission to authority.

After the retreat, during which Stephen sees himself as Lucifer, the fallen angel (an angel has wings like a bird), the bird imagery changes in tone. Wings and birds become images of flight and freedom. The hawklike man flying above the sea in Chapter Four is the symbol of the artist forging a new vision. The girl on the beach is described as a seabird (and angel) with the plumage of a dove. In Chapter Five, immediately following the villanelle passage, birds and bird flight foretell Stephen's own flight to lonely freedom. The message comes "from his heart like a bird from a turret, quietly and swiftly."

Test 2

1. C   **2.** B   **3.** B   **4.** B   **5.** A   **6.** C
7. A   **8.** A   **9.** B   **10.** B

11. In Chapter Five, Davin, MacCann, and Cranly act as devices for revealing Stephen's deeply held opinions. His interaction with them also calls attention to Stephen's difficulty with friendship and love.

The peasant Davin represents the Irish effort to draw new strength from its past ("the sorrowful legend of Ireland") and to rekindle national pride. He is interested in sports, an Irish passion. He tries to teach Gaelic to Stephen and to involve him in national matters. Stephen likes Davin but rejects his efforts to involve him in Irish matters. In doing so, he has a chance to air his criticisms of Ireland.

MacCann is the humanitarian involved in international causes. He believes in universal brotherhood and works hard to improve man's lot. Stephen's refusal to sign MacCann's petitions proves again that he rejects "all enthusiasms." As an artist, he wants to remain uninvolved with causes. By contrast, MacCann's activism serves to underline Stephen's self-absorption.

Cranly serves as neutral listener to Stephen's innermost thoughts. He mainly listens in his role of confessor-analyst. But he too challenges Stephen about his behavior to his mother and his inability to feel the emotion of love.

12. Stephen is profoundly attached to his mother until she objects to his attending the university. Early glimpses of his "nice mother" of the prelude are of a gentle, peacemaking woman. This is her chief role in the Christmas dinner scene. You know how attached Stephen is to her by his fusion of the mother figure with the Blessed Virgin and with his romanticized ideal women. Davin's peasant woman in Chapter Five is a motherly figure (probably pregnant). Even the first prostitute to whom he yields has a motherly aura.

It is Stephen's choice of a university education over a priest's life that causes the "first noiseless sundering" of his attachment to his mother. He feels her faith is getting stronger as his own wanes. It makes her hostile to his university career, which is so exciting for him. In Chapter Five, the burden of his admission to Cranly is that he has refused to do his Easter duty of going to confession before Mass, causing her deep grief. He evades Cranly's question about loving his mother. Yet at the end she is folding her son's clothes, helping to prepare for his departure, which may be a sign that her love for her son exceeds her devotion to religion. Stephen's evasion of Cranly's question suggests that his devotion to his literary destiny exceeds his love for his mother.

13. Words represent power for Stephen. They are the threads that guide him through the maze of his youth. They play an active role; they reveal to Stephen that his destiny is to be a writer.

The first hint of the importance of language is in the childish wordplay of the prelude: "Apologise,/Pull out his eyes." In the first scene at Clongowes, Stephen plays with the words: "belt," "suck." He admires God for being a linguist and understanding all the languages of his flock. Even ordinary sentences from his spelling book sound like poetry. Words can be riddles (Athy's name) and yet solve riddles. They can bring on epiphanies (moments of revelation)—for example, "foetus" in the visit to Cork.

You'll find many instances of the importance of words and wordplay scattered through the book. A key passage in Chapter Four describes the role that words play as a window to the real world. The phrase "a day of dappled seaborne clouds" sets off the moment of revelation in which Stephen sees that his destiny lies in the art of words. He perceives the world of emotion can best be expressed through "a lucid supple periodic prose." On his way to the university, words frolic in his head in whimsical "wayward rhythms." Words fill him with "a soft liquid joy."

14. The girl on the beach is nameless. She is both real and a symbol. Stephen describes her as "the angel of mortal youth." She belongs both to heaven (angel) and to earth (mortal). Stephen will never see her again, but she has marked his life.

The mortal girl is healthy and beautiful. She is feminine without being provocative. She is firm-fleshed and rounded, like a woman, but her face and hair are "girlish." Stephen feels "profane joy" at her sight, but he compares her to a seabird, his new symbol of freedom.

Joyce has scattered symbolic details in his description of the girl, but what she stands for is open to interpretation. Is she a siren (temptress) with a green trail of seaweed, luring Stephen back to a green Ireland? Does green seaweed make her the symbol of Irish womanhood? Her ivory-hued thighs and her slate blue skirts are the colors of the statue of the Blessed Virgin Mary. ("Ivory" also recalls virginal Eileen (Vance) of the pale hands.) The comparison with the dove is thought by some to refer to the dove as symbol of the Holy Ghost that appeared in the sky when Christ was baptized by St. John the Baptist. They see the girl as a heavenly messenger approving Stephen's baptism into the religion of art. Or perhaps she is meant to represent Stephen's muse, the classical, pagan source of artistic inspiration.

You might argue that the girl on the beach represents all of these meanings—the sacred and profane, the real and the romantic, the religious and artistic—since she seems to represent a vision of perfect unity for Stephen.

Term Paper Ideas and other Topics for Writing

Themes

1. What does the pandying episode contribute to Stephen's view of life? Of priests?

2. Why is Stephen critical of Ireland? Why does he choose to live in continental Europe?

3. Explain the meaning of Stephen's choice of "the misrule and confusion of his father's house" over the orderly life of a priest.

4. Discuss the relationship between the pagan myth of Daedalus and the Christian version of the fall of both Adam and Lucifer.

5. How do the commands to "apologise," "confess," and "admit," work throughout *Portrait of the Artist* to express different kinds of conformity?

Characters

1. What is Heron's role in Stephen's life?

2. Are Stephen's growing pains different from the usual ones of adolescence? If so, how do they differ?

3. What kind of man is Simon Dedalus, and why does Stephen feel alienated from him?

4. Discuss *Portrait of the Artist* as a negative portrait of Stephen.

Literary Topics

1. What did Joyce admire about Henrik Ibsen? How does *Portrait of the Artist* reflect Ibsen's influence?

2. Compare *Portrait of the Artist* with either Somerset Maugham's *Of Human Bondage* or with D.H. Lawrence's *Sons and Lovers*.

3. Discuss Joyce's attitude toward W.B. Yeats and the Irish literary revival movement as reflected in *Portrait of the Artist*.

Literary Technique

1. How does the style of *Portrait of the Artist* change during the stages of Stephen's growing up?

2. Discuss Joyce's use of language to break down the traditional barriers among the five senses.

3. How does Joyce adapt his style to his subject matter in contrasting Stephen's view of reality with his romantic dreams?

4. How is the image of water and wetness used to reveal aspects of Stephen's character?

5. What does the structure of *Portrait of the Artist* have in common with the classical drama of ancient Greece or with the typical nineteenth-century symphony?

6. Discuss the way Joyce uses the rose as a motif.

Further Reading
CRITICAL WORKS

Anderson, Chester G., ed. *James Joyce, A Portrait of the Artist as a Young Man: Text, Criticism and Notes.* New York: Penguin, 1982. Indispensable, close analysis of *Portrait* text. Includes excerpts from *Stephen Hero* and critical essays.

Bolt, Sydney. *A Preface to James Joyce*. London and New York: Longman, 1981. Compact background material and critical survey.

Bowen, Zack, and James F. Carens, eds. *A Companion to Joyce Studies*. Westport, Conn.: Greenwood, 1984. Includes an exhaustive discussion of plot, themes, and structural devices.

Chace, William, ed. *Joyce: A Collection of Critical Essays*. Englewood Cliffs, N.J.: Prentice Hall, 1976.

Connolly, Thomas E., ed. *Joyce's Portrait: Criticisms and Critiques*. New York: Appleton-Century-Crofts, 1962.

Ellmann, Richard. *James Joyce*. Rev. ed. Oxford and New York: Oxford University Press, 1982. A definitive biography.

Gifford, Don. *Joyce Annotated: Notes for "Dubliners" and "A Portrait of the Artist as a Young Man."* Berkeley and Los Angeles: University of California Press, 1982. Excellent source for Irish background.

Gross, John. *James Joyce*. New York: Viking, 1970. A balanced appraisal.

Joyce, Stanislaus. *My Brother's Keeper*. New York: Viking, 1958. A first-hand report on the Joyce family by James' younger brother.

Levin, Harry. *James Joyce: A Critical Introduction*. (Revised and augmented edition) New York: New Directions, 1960. A classic appraisal by an outstanding Joyce scholar.

Magalaner, Marvin, and Richard M. Kain. *Joyce: The Man, the Work, the Reputation*. New York: New York University Press, 1956. Valuable appraisal of Joyce at mid-century.

Ryf, Robert S. *A New Approach to Joyce*. Berkeley and Los Angeles: University of California Press, 1964. Lively analysis of *Portrait* as a microcosm of all of Joyce's work.

Tindall, William York. *A Reader's Guide to James Joyce*.

New York: Octagon, 1971. Good introduction to Joyce
    for the general reader.
Wright, David G. *Characters of Joyce.* New York: Barnes
    & Noble, 1983.

AUTHOR'S OTHER WORKS

1907	*Chamber Music* (poetry)
1914	*Dubliners* (stories)
1918	*Exiles* (play)
1922	*Ulysses* (novel)
1927	*Pomes Penyeach* (poetry)
1936	*Collected Poems* (includes *Chamber Music*, *Pomes Penyeach* and an additional volume, *Ecce Puer*)
1939	*Finnegans Wake* (novel)
1957–1966	*Letters of James Joyce*, vols. 1, 2, and 3 (vol. 1 ed. by S. Gilbert, revised by R. Ellmann; vols. 2 and 3 ed. by R. Ellmann)
1959	*Critical Writings of James Joyce* (ed. by E. Mason and R. Ellmann)
1963	*Stephen Hero* (novel)
1968	*Giacomo Joyce* (short story)
1975	*Selected Letters of James Joyce* (ed. by R. Ellmann)

(*Stephen Hero* and *Giacomo Joyce* were published post-
humously.)

Glossary

Ally Daly   Slang for "tops," the very best.
Amana   Mountains in biblical Lebanon, mentioned in
    Old Testament Canticle of Canticles (Song of Solo-
    mon).

Bake "In a great bake" means "hot under the collar."

Ballocks Slang word for testicles; also a clumsy oaf.

Bective Rangers A leading Irish football team. (Irish football combines elements of soccer and rugby.)

Black and Tans Nickname for British (and Irish) soldiers used against Irish revolutionaries after World War I.

Black twist Longleaf tobacco twisted into a thick cord for smoking.

Bowling Word used for "pitching" in cricket, a ball and bat game popular in the British Isles.

Byron, Lord (1788–1824) English romantic poet, famous as much for his turbulent personal life as for his writing.

Cachou Candy made from cashew nuts.

The Castle Main building complex at Clongowes where the rector's office was located.

Cavalcanti, Guido 13th-century Italian poet known for his lyrical poetry.

Chasuble Sleeveless outer garment worn by a priest celebrating Mass.

Ciborium Goblet-shaped vessel holding the wafers (bread) used in the Communion service.

Cod Slang for a joke or prank.

"Come-all-yous" Popular street ballad.

Davitt, Michael (1846–1906) Leader, with Charles Stewart Parnell, of Irish land reform movement. Split with Parnell over reform theory and refused to support him after the O'Shea scandal.

Dilectus Collection of Latin quotations.

Drisheen Stuffed intestine dish characteristic of County Cork.

Elements Most elementary level of Clongowes school.

Feck To fetch or to steal.

Fenians Members of Sinn Féin, a radical Irish nationalist movement. "Fianna!" was their rallying cry.

Firbolgs and Milesians Legendary early inhabitants of

Ireland. Firbolgs were described as crude, short, and dark, Milesians as artistic, tall, and handsome.

Gaelic League Group founded in 1893 to revive the Irish language and Irish traditions.

Hauptmann, Gerhart (1862–1946) German dramatist, novelist, and poet, whose later work blended romanticism and realism.

Healy, Timothy Michael (1855–1931) Irish nationalist and Charles Stewart Parnell's right-hand man, who eventually broke with him in 1886 over Home Rule policy.

Hurling Fast, rough Irish game like hockey and lacrosse. "Minding the cool" is guarding the goal. A "camaun" or "camán" is used (like a hockey stick) to advance the ball.

Ironing room Storage room for armor in a medieval castle.

Ibsen, Henrik (1828–1906) Norwegian playwright, called the father of modern drama. His plays use both realism and symbolism to probe conflicts.

Jackeen Lower-class Dubliner.

Jingle Two-wheeled, covered, horse-drawn cart.

Kentish fire Disapproval expressed by prolonged foot-stomping or hand-clapping.

L.D.S. Acronym of *Laus Deo Semper*, Latin for *praise to God Always*; placed at end of written school work in Jesuit schools.

Lob Money or something valuable.

Loft Place where punishments were meted out at Belvedere College.

Mallarmé, Stéphane (1842–1898) Leader of the French Symbolist school of poetry, which used words as symbols to suggest nuances of meaning.

Maneens Dialect word for "little men."

Mardyke Once-fashionable promenade (walkway) in the city of Cork.

Marryat, Captain Frederick (1792–1848) English Navy officer who wrote novels about sea life and other adventure books popular with boys.

Muff Slang for a novice, fool, or clumsy fellow.

Pandybat Leather strap reinforced with whalebone; used at Clongowes to strike boys on their palms as a punishment.

Parnell, Charles Stewart (1846–1891) Popular Irish leader and member of the British Parliament where he championed Irish agrarian reform and Home Rule. He fell from power after his adulterous relationship with Mrs. Kitty O'Shea was made public.

Paten Plate used to hold the wafers (bread) in the Communion service.

Pater, Walter (1839–1894) British essayist who dominated literary criticism in the 1890s. He held that the role of the artist was to create personal artistic expressions rather than to provide moral or social uplift.

Peach on Slang for inform against, tattle.

Plucked Student slang for "flunked."

Prefect In English and Irish secondary schools, a student monitor. Less often, a teacher.

Rounders Game similar to baseball.

Seraphim Highest of the nine orders of angels.

Sinn Féin ("We Ourselves") Irish nationalist party, dating from 1902, which opposed English rule moderately at first, but became more radical after the Dublin Easter uprising in 1916.

Six and Eight Total number of punishment strokes of the pandybat on each hand; three on each hand, followed by four.

Slim Jim Strip of candy.

Soutane Long gown of a priest worn during services.

Square School urinal at Clongowes.

Sugar or **sugan** A rope made of twisted straw; therefore, a term for a weak person.

Swinburne, Algernon Charles (1837–1909)   English poet whose verses were musical, sensuous, and often erotic.

Symons, Arthur (1865–1945)   British poet and critic who championed the French Symbolist movement, and followed the precepts of Walter Pater.

Tantiles   Loiterers.

Tara   Site in County Meath, Ireland, important in Irish legend and history as center of third-century kingdom; Camelot in British legend and history.

Tennyson, Alfred, Lord (1809–1892)   Poet laureate of England, whose immensely popular work expressed the predominant moral and social values of the Victorian era. He was later criticized for being overly sentimental and narrow-minded.

Thurible   Church vessel in which incense is burned.

Tolka   Small river north of Dublin. Tolka cottages were mud huts.

Tone (Theobald) Wolfe (1763–1798)   Eighteenth-century Irish patriot and revolutionary who founded the Society of United Irishmen with Hamilton Rowan and James Napper Tandy. Their goal was to unite Protestant and Catholic Ireland into an independent and secular republic.

Waistcoateers   Elizabethan English word for prostitutes.

Yeats, William Butler (1865–1939)   Leading Irish modern poet and dramatist, and a leader of the Irish literary revival called the Irish Renaissance. He used Irish folklore and history in much of his work.

The Critics

Portrait of the Artist as Autobiography

All these ironies, mild as they are, remind us again that Stephen is not Joyce and that there is a comic dimension to the *Portrait*, all the stronger because

Stephen is unaware of it. Stephen's life resembles
Joyce's but he is displaced, living in a different and
more sombre environment. He is less happy, more
troubled, than Joyce; he is surrounded by people
less substantial than Joyce's associates were and
consequently seems less intellectually agile and more
isolated. The world mocks his attempts to attain
maturity and individuality. Joyce presents Stephen's ideas seriously enough but undercuts them
by showing their limitations, questioning whether
Stephen understands their full meaning and partly
avoiding them while writing the novel in which they
appear.

—*David G. Wright*, Characters of
Joyce, 1983

Portrait of the Artist vs. *Stephen Hero*

Had Joyce died after writing *A Portrait of the Artist
as a Young Man* his reputation as a novelist of stature
could have rested on that one work alone. Its flaws
. . . are faults which a long work in prose may over-
ride as a poem may not; and the *Portrait* does,
triumphantly. Yet it has rarely received its due. Interest in it as a novel has been dissipated by its
obvious autobiographical content. . . . Of all Joyce's
works the *Portrait* has suffered most from this dis-
trust of the constructive intellect in art. The existence of an earlier version, *Stephen Hero*, undisci-
plined and extravagant of detail, has induced a
general easy acquiescence in the view that the *Portrait*
is by comparison, deliberate, artificial and cold-
blooded. It does not in fact lack feeling. Its inspiration is to be traced to far more profound and
integrated experiences than anything behind the
adolescent *Stephen Hero*. . . .

The earlier novel is a straightforward naturalistic
narrative, comprehensive, frank, humorous and
partisan. . . . *Stephen Hero* does present a picture of
the hero and his notions on art, but it is set against
a very rich background of family, friends, city and
religion—a family consisting of father, mother, a
brother who is a close friend, a sister and minor
relatives, friends who have distinct personalities and

whose opinions are not only independent of Stephen but important to him; Dublin, which is both a city and a language; and Catholicism as religion and the channel of education. . . . [T]he earlier draft is a study of a son and a brother, of a very human though consciously clever and eccentric student, at once painfully and happily growing into a writer. The *Portrait*, on the other hand, is the work of an accomplished artist creating directly out of the experiences and responsibilities of his calling.

> —*Jane H. Jack,* "Art and *A Portrait of the Artist,*" 1955; reprinted in Thomas Connolly, *Joyce's Portrait*, 1962.

Stephen the Egotist

Confronted with these responses and questions, one would have to admit that the Stephen Dedalus who sets forth in the novel's last lines "to forge in the smithy of my soul the uncreated conscience of my race" is a preposterous egotist who has little to show for all the extravagance of his ambition. Stephen has not developed an aesthetic philosophy. Had he done so, one would have to insist that Joyce had created the most untypical brilliant undergraduate of the world's literature. As it is, one can grant that, out of need and largely to justify himself, Stephen has expressed some brilliant but not necessarily consistent insights. Stephen may have enrolled in the priesthood of art, but, again, one must admit that it would be difficult to describe him as a poet on the basis of his villanelle. On the other hand, granting every irony that has been claimed for the way Joyce depicts the composition of the poem and every criticism that has been made of its *fin de siècle* affectation, it can be affirmed that the villanelle is the work of an undergraduate of undeniable talent.

> —*Zack Bowen and James F. Carens,* eds. A Companion to Joyce Studies, *1984*

Stephen's Promise as a Writer

. . . the *Portrait* is surely meant to leave us with equivocal feelings about its hero's potentialities. For

much of the time Stephen embodies an aspect of
Joyce's nature that he repeatedly punished in his
books but that he could never finally quell: the
egoarch, the poseur with a smack of Hamlet, the
narcissist who dedicated his first extended work (a
play written at the age of eighteen and subsequently
lost) "to My own Soul." But he also represents Joyce
by virtue of his unaccommodating ideals and his
restless imagination: even the purple patches hold
out the promise of a more authentic, more distinc-
tive lyricism. And he has the courage of his im-
maturity, which means having the capacity to grow
and change, of not being afraid of a plunge into the
unknown. Whether he will ultimately justify his
presumptuousness and succeed in writing his masterpiece is an open question as the book ends.
—*John Gross*, James Joyce, *1970*

Joyce's Visual Sense

Harry Levin has characterized Joyce's writing as being
of "low visibility," his imagination as being auditory rather than visual, and his most direct concern
being with the ear rather than the eye. . . .

No one would deny that Joyce had poor eyesight,
keen ears, was preoccupied with language, and frequently used musical forms and effects in his writing. But the premise that poor eyesight inevitably
results in writing strong in auditory imagery and
weak in visual imagery does not prove itself. The
impairment of one sense does not necessarily result
in a diminished artistic representation of that sense.
Beethoven is an obvious example. . . . The demon-
strable fact is that Joyce was thoroughly at home
with the visual, and relied on it to achieve some of
his most telling and important effects. In the *Portrait*
we have on the one hand the images clustering
around the conformity-authority-punishment axis—
the moocow, eagles pulling out eyes, the pandybat.
Then there are the images that represent the wooing
and winning of Stephen to a life of artistic creativity—the intricate pattern of hand-and-arm imagery,
the apparition of the hawklike man flying sunward
over the sea, the girl on the beach, and Stephen's

vision of the unfolding flower. This is only a brief listing of the motifs or images that address themselves directly to the eye. Clearly, they indicate a visual imagination on the part of their creator. The failure to appreciate this fact inevitably robs the reader, and results in an unbalanced or one-dimensional view of Joyce.

—*Robert S. Ryf,* A New Approach to Joyce, *1964*

Joyce's Language

Joyce's own contribution to English prose is to provide a more fluid medium for refracting sensations and impressions through the author's mind—to facilitate the transition from photographic realism to esthetic impressionism. In the introductory pages of the *Portrait of the Artist,* the reader is faced with nothing less than the primary impact of life itself, a presentational continuum of the tastes and smells and sights and sounds of earliest infancy. Emotion is integrated, from first to last, by words. Feelings, as they filter through Stephen's sensory apparatus, become associated with phrases. His conditioned reflexes are literary. . . .

This is the state of mind that confers upon language a magical potency. It exalts the habit of verbal association into a principle for the arrangement of experience. You gain power over a thing by naming it; you become master of a situation by putting it into words. It is psychological need, and not hyperfastidious taste, that goads the writer on to search for the *mot juste,* to loot the thesaurus.

—*Harry Levin,* James Joyce: A Critical Introduction, *1960*

NOTES